SHARING JESUS WITH
UNDER FIVES

This book is dedicated to my parents,
Dick and Rosalind Moser, with love
and gratitude for the strong foundations
they built in my life.

SHARING JESUS WITH UNDER FIVES

JANET GAUKROGER

CROSSWAY BOOKS
NOTTINGHAM

ISBN 1–85684–087–5

Unless otherwise stated, Scripture quotations in this
publication are from the Holy Bible, New International
Version. Copyright © 1973, 1978, 1984 International Bible
Society. Published in Great Britain by Hodder &
Stoughton Ltd.

Typeset by Avocet Type, Bicester, Oxon.
Printed in Great Britain for Crossway Books,
Norton Street, Nottingham NG7 3HR,
by Cox & Wyman Ltd, Reading, Berkshire.

Contents

Introduction

My first experience of teaching under fives at church was probably about sixteen years ago. My mother has taught various ages under five ever since I can remember, and it was in answer to a need for a teacher of three-year-olds that I first became involved. Little did I know then that it would lead to this!

In twelve years of marriage to Steve I have had the opportunity to be in many churches up and down the country. My involvement with the Baptist Union, Spring Harvest, and other conferences brings me into contact with people from churches of every description. In the last several years two things have struck me time and time again as I talk with folk in these settings.

Firstly, it seems that a growing number of churches are realizing that they could be doing more with their under fives than they have in the past. Almost every time someone discovers that I am responsible for organizing Christian education for under fives at Stopsley, they ask me what we do, how we do it, where we get material and so on.

Secondly, I find a large number of Christian parents who love the Lord and want to pass the faith on to their children. But they have no idea how to go about it. Many are largely unaware of how children develop emotionally and spiritually, and do not know what things they can teach them as a foundation for later commitment.

It is these things in combination which have prompted the writing of this book. I am concerned to see that as churches we do not miss any opportunity to help our children grow up with a love for, and commitment to, the Word of God and the local church. The battle for the next generation is largely won when they are young.

I am also concerned that we, as Christian parents, give our children the best foundation possible in the things of

God. I want my children to grow up with a living, vibrant faith. I do not just want to teach them the right things to do, I want to show them how to know the Lord, and love him joyfully.

If you are a parent, I pray that as you read this book you will be thrilled with the potential of passing on the faith to your children. I hope you will find it practical and helpful.

If you are concerned with the under fives in your church, I pray that you will find a strong basis for teaching, as well as many useful suggestions for working it out in practice.

At the end of the Lord's Prayer we say, 'Your kingdom come, your will be done'. As we teach the things of God to our children, may we see his Kingdom come, in our own lives, and for the next generation.

Chapter 1

Why teach the under fives?

Anyone who has been a parent or has had anything to do with young children knows that they can learn. Not only that, they are constantly learning, even when we are not consciously teaching. In the twentieth century there has been an explosion of studies relating to human development, and a number of theories concerned with the way humans learn. Although the minute detail of reports would vary, the overwhelming conclusion of the research is that a child learns and develops more in the first five years of life than in any other comparable time span.

Think about it: Babies are born into the world quite helpless and totally dependent on others to meet their needs. Their 'speech' is limited to crying and gurgling, and in the first few days of life, the only purposeful bodily movement they are capable of is sucking.

By the age of five, they are able to walk, run, jump, skip and hop. They can feed themselves, dress themselves, and they have control over their bodily functions. Their ability to communicate through speech, gesture, and even facial expression is well developed.

The massive developmental progress of the first five years is not limited only to the mental and physical aspects of life. It also occurs in the realm of the emotional/social and moral/spiritual.

When children are born, they are capable of seeing the world only from their own point of view. They are totally egocentric, not because they choose to be, but because they are not yet in possession of the mental processes that allow them to consider how other people might feel.

By the age of five, they are well established in the lifelong process of learning to work and play with others. They are learning about acting and making decisions as a result not only of their own needs and wants, but the concerns of others as well.

By the time children are five their social patterns (ways of dealing with and handling people), their self-esteem (feelings about themselves), and their general view of life are already well developed. Their basic personality, though not completely set, is already gelling. Many of their character traits will persist for a lifetime barring some dramatic (positive) or traumatic (negative) intervention.

On the surface this can look like pretty bad news. Does this mean that for all of us with children over five it is already too late? Does it mean that our failings as adults are outside our control, a result of mis-setting of our personalities all those years ago? No, of course not! If that were so, the future would look rather bleak, and there would be no hope for improvement.

As Christians, we have given our lives over to the God who can change anything. Of our own accord, we cannot do much to change all that is wrong in our lives. But God has made his power available to us, so that by his love and grace we can become the people he longs for us to be.

So, where does all this leave us? Any discussion of what we should or shouldn't do with under fives must be set in the context of realizing how much children are taking in in those first years, and how all that they experience shapes the people they become. In the middle section of this book we will take a more in-depth look at child development, and at what tasks children master at various stages. We will look at their emotional and spiritual development, and at how what we do or don't do affects them.

For now, though, we have set the scene for beginning to answer the question, 'Why teach the under fives?'

Everything that children see, hear, taste, touch and smell in the first few years of life is laying foundations for how they understand themselves, others, and the world around them. The experiences they have in those pre-school years shape lifelong attitudes. Young children are like sponges, soaking up all that they are told, and all that they perceive about what goes on around them.

If this is the case, it would seem that the early years are the ideal time for beginning to communicate the truths of the Christian faith. By teaching these truths from the time a child is born, we are making the most of receptive minds and spirits. Of course, every person reaches the stage where they must make their own personal response to God, but many people are unable to do this because they have never known anything of the God who loves them.

I once read a statement that went something like this: 'Why teach a young child about Jesus? So that on that day when he is old enough to understand what Jesus did for him on the cross, he won't have any trouble accepting the Jesus he has known about all his life'. It isn't always that straightforward, but I am absolutely committed to the principle expressed in that statement.

Looking at the church in Britain today, it seems that most of our time is spent trying to redeem a godless generation. We have to start at square one with most adults, helping them to understand that there is a God who loves them, and that he wants to have a relationship with them.

Once they have come to a personal faith in Jesus, it may require hours of counselling, and months, or even years, of prayer to undo the damage done in their lives and to bring their personalities in line with what God wants them to be.

Please don't misunderstand what I am saying. Of course, every person is loved and valued by God, and is worth our utmost efforts to enable them to be whole. And for all of us, whatever our background, it takes a lifetime of prayer to continue the journey towards being like Jesus.

We will always need to pour a great deal of time and effort into rescuing men and women from darkness and bringing them into God's marvellous light. Not only that, it is vital that we are committed to doing the same with

11

young people and children, through evangelism and practical care.

But what if, as those who already know and love the Lord, we put more thought and effort into passing on the faith to our children from the day they are born? What if we were to see a generation of children who have grown up never knowing anything but to love the Lord? What if from their earliest days we helped them to build the truths of the Bible into their personalities? What if, when they reached the age of making their own commitment to God, it was a natural step? They would already have such a grounding in the faith that Bible study, prayer, lifestyle, evangelism, and being part of the church family would simply be follow-ons to all that they already know. The impact on the kingdom of God and on his church would be enormous. What an exciting thought!

I believe that what we do with under fives at church (and at home!) is absolutely vital. Teaching them the things of God from the very beginning is seizing a valuable opportunity that we will never again have in the same way. Communicating biblical truths in ways that are appropriate to their stage of development and understanding means that they will learn.

The other side of that truth is that failure to teach at church means that they still learn. What they learn is that what Mum and Dad go to church for isn't important for them, that it is something for grown-ups. They learn that church is not a particularly fun place to be. They learn that church is a place where they are not really wanted. They switch off when they get inside – and once they switch off, it is difficult to get them to switch on again. Even very young children have an amazing ability to sense mood and atmosphere. They know when they are valued and they know when they are not!

Jesus valued children. Which of us is not familiar with the story in Matthew 19? The disciples rebuked the parents for 'bothering' Jesus with their children. But Jesus said and did something very important for those children (and, no doubt, their parents!) that day. He demonstrated his love for them by taking time for them, by showing affection to them, and by blessing them.

Jesus also had some very strong words of warning for those who cause young ones to 'stumble'. In Matthew 18 he says, '. . . it would be better for him to have a large millstone hung around his neck and to be drowned in the depths of the sea' (verse 6). Sometimes we cause children to stumble by the things we say and do. But I believe we can also cause them to stumble by the things we do not say and do. We know that we cannot guarantee that our children will grow up to accept the faith which is ours as their parents. But what a tragedy if they reject it because we did not take the opportunity to teach them when they were young.

The Apostle Paul instructed his fellow Christians to live wisely, making the most of the time. He obviously thought it was important, because he said it to two different groups, the Ephesians (chapter five) and the Colossians (chapter four). As Christians in today's world, we cannot afford the luxury of wasted time and effort for God. We must seek his wisdom so that we will, indeed, make the most of the time and opportunities we have.

I believe that the under fives present us with a very significant opportunity. We can affect the next generation for good and for God by passing on the faith now to our little ones. There is an urgency about this task. The years in which they are so receptive to all that we would want to teach them are few. The pressures that they face from 'outside' come so quickly, that we must pour our love for God and his Word into their young lives while we can.

In the film *Dead Poet's Society*, the teacher (played by Robin Williams) has a favourite expression, *carpe diem* – seize the day. What an appropriate word for us as Christians at the end of the twentieth century. There are many opportunities that we must make the most of. Teaching the under fives is one of them.

My husband found a poem a few years ago which sums up the importance of prevention, rather than cure. It is relevant to many areas of our lives and work as Christians.

'Twas a dangerous cliff, as they freely
     confessed,
Though to walk near its crest was so
     pleasant;
But over its terrible edge there had
     slipped
A Duke and full many a peasant.

So the people said something would have
     to be done,
But their project did not at all tally;
Some said, 'Put a fence round the edge of
     the cliff.'
Some said, 'An ambulance down in the
     valley.'

And the cry for an ambulance carried the
     day,
For it spread to a neighbouring city.
A fence may be useful or not, it is true,
But each heart became brim full of pity –

For those who slipped over the terrible
     cliff.
And the dwellers in highway and alley
Gave pounds or gave pence, not to put
     up a fence
But an ambulance down in the valley.

'For the cliff is alright, if you're careful,'
     they said,
'And if folks ever slip and are dropping,
It isn't the slipping that hurts them so
     much
As the shock down below when they're
     stopping!'

So day after day, as the mishaps
     occurred,
Quick forth would rescuers sally,

To pick up the victims who fell from the
  cliff,
With an ambulance down in the valley.

Better guard well the young than reclaim
  them when old,
For the voice of true wisdom is calling;
To rescue the fallen is good, but 'tis best
To prevent other people from falling.

Better close up the source of temptation
  and crime
Than deliver from dungeon and galley;
Better build a strong fence round the top
  of the cliff,
Than an ambulance down in the valley!

Teaching the under fives raises many questions. How do
we teach them? What do we teach them? When do we
teach them? The following sections will deal with both the
theory and the practice of passing on the faith to the under
fives. Hopefully, they will provide some answers to these
questions.

Chapter 2
Attitudes to children

A little boy was confused by the constant barrage of 'don'ts' he received at church. 'You mustn't shout (run, play, laugh, etc.) in God's house.' Finally he was heard to ask, 'Doesn't God like little children?'

As we begin to think through the whole area of passing on the faith to the under fives, it may be helpful to begin with a look at the church's attitude to young children in general. In these days of computer technology we are becoming familiar with a whole new vocabulary of terms. A very popular phrase in many settings is 'user-friendly'. This concept is now applied in a wide variety of situations, including the church. A large number of churches are asking themselves whether they are user-friendly to visitors and non-Christians. This is a helpful exercise if it moves us on to making our presentation of the good news of Jesus more relevant to the communities in which we minister.

Another question that is being asked by more and more churches is 'Are we children-friendly?', or in this case, 'Are we under fives-friendly?' Sadly the answer is often a resounding 'no!' Perhaps we should ask this question of the under fives themselves. In her very helpful book, *Under Fives and their Families*, Judith Wigley asks the question 'How do our under fives see the church on a Sunday?'

I suspect that if a toddling two-year-old were able to write to their grandparents concerning their first visit to church it might read a little like this:

Dear Grandma,
   This morning Mummy took me to church for the very first time. I thought we were going to

Rainbow Toddlers because we went through the big giant's door but we weren't because the room was different and much bigger. It was cold, with nothing on the floor and we didn't take our coats off all the time we were there.

There was a man at the door who didn't know Mummy but he sort of smiled at her. She got a book and a piece of paper. I don't think he saw me because I didn't get anything, only the grown-ups did.

Auntie Joan was there from toddlers and my special friend Lucy. Lucy wasn't allowed to sit by me because she was with her Daddy and big sister. Our Daddy didn't want to come. I stood up on the seat to wave to Lucy but her Daddy told her to sit down and be good. I only wanted to wave. The lady behind us asked Mummy to take me off the seat because I was making it dirty so she carried me. I wanted to see the man who was talking.

Soon we started to play games. First it was dressing up but only the men at the front were allowed to play. It wasn't fair really because I wanted to put on a big dress like them. We all played hide-and-seek though, grandma, even the grown-ups. You get down and hide behind the seat, and when the man says the magic word 'Amen' you jump up again. They played that three times!

Singing time was good fun but I didn't know all the songs. They sang some that we sing in Rainbow Toddlers, clapping and dancing songs. There was a big space for dancing and jumping right between the seats but nobody used it. It was hard to dance in Mummy's arms but I made a big noise clapping. Lucy did too but her Daddy told her to be quiet. Grandma, can you clap quietly? The grown-ups were very good at it in church.

> *You have to pay to go to church, Grandma. Two men came round with big plates and collected all your money. Some people didn't have any money so they gave them an envelope instead. But you know something, Grandma, you didn't get any drinks and biscuits after you'd paid. They just gave it all to the man at the front. I think that he must be very rich.*
>
> *Later the man at the front said all the children had to go out, I think he was fed up of us . . .*
>
> *. . . At the end, the man dressed up was standing by the door. He asked Mummy if she had been before and said he hoped that she would come again. He shook Mummy's hand. He didn't speak to me, I don't think he wants me to come again. Perhaps it's because I can't clap quietly or because I wanted to wave to Lucy. I didn't mean to dirty the seat, Grandma — I only wanted to see.*
>
> *. . . I'm not sure if I want to go again.*
>
> *Lots of love, Jannie XXXX* [1]

We have already said that children are always learning, even when we are not consciously teaching. We need to ask ourselves what they are learning when they come through the doors of the church on Sunday. Many young children attend playgroups or crèches during the week where the equipment and activities are designed to meet their needs. How sad if they come to church on Sunday to find that not only is nothing geared to their needs, but no one even seems to know what their needs are.

We must examine carefully our attitudes towards under fives in the church. Many of us still operate on the

[1] Wigley, Judith. *Under Fives and their Families.* A CPAS Handbook (Marshall Pickering, 1990), p. 88.

old adage 'Children should be seen and not heard'. Some of us might want to add, 'and preferably not even seen!'

Other churches are much more progressive than this. They are not against children – but they are not in favour of them, either! Some may feel that since children are 'the church of tomorrow' we had better put up with them today. Others respond on a much more practical level – 'Help! We've got all these little children. What are we supposed to do with them?'

What should our attitude be? Is there a biblically correct position concerning the under fives?

I don't think we will find in the pages of Scripture a practical guide for what we should be doing with under fives. (If we could, I wouldn't be writing this book, and you wouldn't need to read it!) What we will find, though, are principles which will guide our attitudes. When we have godly attitudes we will then be able to work out the most acceptable practice for our situation.

In Psalm 139 we see that every individual is made and intimately known by God. The whole book of Psalms abounds with references to God's steadfast love. The Bible leaves us in no doubt about God's intense love for every person. I find nothing in Scripture which indicates that he values adults more highly than children, or vice versa. God's love for each one of us surpasses anything we can imagine. Paul's prayer for the Ephesians, in chapter three, is that they may somehow grasp the length, width, depth and height of Christ's love, so that they may be filled with the fullness of God. We know that God loves us completely, young and old alike.

We also know that we must love one another. In I John chapter three, we are told that 'this is the message you heard from the beginning: We should love one another' (verse 11). John goes on to say that we should lay down our lives for one another, and love not only with words but also with actions. In Philippians, chapter two, Paul exhorts us to 'look not only to your own interests, but also to the interests of others' (verse 4). I see no reason to think that these commands should apply only to the adults in the family of God. In fact, most of us as Christian parents would be teaching our children to follow such commands. How many of us have told our children that the Bible says, 'Be kind and compassionate to one another' (Ephesians 4:32) and then have failed to show that same kindness and compassion to the children in our care? These rules concerning our attitudes to one another apply not only in adult/adult relationships, but also in adult/child relationships.

So we are sure of God's love for every individual, and we want to take seriously the command to look to the interests of others. How does that work out in our attitude to the under fives in our church? It means that we will see them as part of the church family today, not just tomorrow. It means that as we strive to meet the needs of adults in the church, we will strive to meet their needs, too. It means that, just as we see adults as contributing members of the body, we see that children have something to offer, too. Judith Wigley reminds us that:

> . . . children teach us many of the realities and truths of the Kingdom of God – they are living examples of dependency and trust, with a quickness to forgive, and so on, traits which Jesus so clearly commended. Without the contribution of these members we are in danger of missing out and being an incomplete body. We are one body called to serve one another, and in so doing we will learn about the grace and knowledge of our God.[2]

She also says, most helpfully:

> Babies and small children are 'dependent' members of the body of Christ, just as old, sick or disabled members of our congregation are too. There will always be such dependent members of the body and therefore always a need for the body to accept a responsibility towards this group of people. It doesn't mean that they cannot contribute or that they have nothing to offer, but simply that they are dependent upon the body for their contribution to be of value or use.[3]

This attitude towards children may look good on paper, and sound right biblically. The problem is putting it into practice! Isn't that true of so much of what the Bible tells us? The idea of loving one another, of sharing our faith, of using our gifts in the body all sounds good. The point at which most of us get stuck is actually doing it! But if

---

[2] Wigley, Judith. *Under Fives and their Families*, p. 91.
[3] *Ibid.*, p. 91.

the principle is right, we must find a way to make it work practically.

Chapter 3

What about parents?

Before planning a strategy and developing a programme for under fives, it is important to consider their parents and the homes from which they come. Children should not be seen in isolation, but as members of their families, and as part of the church family. This raises a number of issues.

The balance of home and church

We ought to say from the beginning that the primary responsibility for spiritual training of children rests with the home. This is certainly the pattern in the Old Testament. What we know of Jewish history tells us that much knowledge was handed down from one generation to the next by word of mouth. Telling and retelling of stories that explained God's dealings with his people, and memorization of the laws he had given them were essential to the passing on of the faith. God had instructed the people early on that they should observe all his commands and decrees so that they, their children, and their children after them would fear the Lord. In Deuteronomy we find this command:

> Love the LORD your God with all your heart and with all your soul and with all your strength. These commandments that I give you today are to be upon your hearts. Impress them on your children. Talk about them when you sit at home and when you walk along the road, when you lie down and when you get up. Tie them as symbols on your hands and bind them on your foreheads. Write them on the door-frames of your houses and on your gates. (Dt. 6:5–9)

Clearly it was God's intention that the passing on of the faith was to be a natural part of everyday life. You can almost imagine a Jewish father or mother talking with their children as they worked in the field or in the home. They would tell them the stories of Abraham, Isaac and Jacob, and of all the wilderness wanderings. You can see them sitting round the fire in the evening, and a child saying, 'Tell us again about the time the waters parted and the people crossed the Red Sea'. In those days, when people's homes were not lined with bookshelves, the only way of teaching and of passing on information was by word of mouth.

It was imperative that adults talked with children about the things of God. Because the family was not defined just in terms of one set of parents with their own children, the whole extended family shared the task of training the children. Grandparents, uncles, aunts and older cousins all joined in the care of children physically, and the nurturing of their faith.

The same command applies to us today. Of course, our way of life is very different from that of the ancient Jews. But the principles God has outlined for his people then are just as valid and essential now. Our responsibility is to work out those principles in the context of modern life.

The traditional concept of the nuclear family (dad at work, mum at home, and 2.4 children happily playing with the dog) is almost completely gone from Western society at the end of the twentieth century. The support and relationships found in the extended family are unknown to most people. So how do we apply God's command to pass on the faith?

This is where the home and the church work together. Whatever the make-up of the home, it is still the primary teacher in the things of God. A home may be defined as the people who are a family by reason of birth, marriage, adoption or invitation. That covers just about every combination we see today! The Christian adults in the home, whoever they may be, take the lead in instructing the children in the faith. The church acts as the extended family, supporting them in that task.

The church can provide spiritual input and experiences that the home cannot provide. Likewise, the home is the proving ground for all that is taught, in the out-working of everyday life and relationships.

The responsibility is great on both sides. No matter how good a church's teaching programme is, one or two hours of input every week are unlikely to make much difference if the same principles are not upheld in the home.

In the same way, if a child is learning and growing in his knowledge of God at home, and he goes to church, only to find that he is not really welcome, or that it is boring, what will that say to him? If he is put in a dark, damp room, with a few tatty toys and adults who never mention the name of Jesus to him, what does he learn? If it doesn't throttle his fledgling faith, it will, at the very least, cause him to think that God is okay but the church is not! So the home and the church must be in partnership.

Support for struggling parents

With the general breakdown of society, and the specific breakdown of family relationships, many parents of young children find themselves really struggling. Even in those Christian homes where the marriage is stable, mums and dads can feel they are floundering for direction. They have questions about discipline, education and spiritual life. Many adults in our churches grew up in homes where the examples set for them of marriage and parenting were indifference, quarrelling, or physical or sexual abuse. Their faith in Christ is real and they are maturing in discipleship. But when they get married or have children, they find that they have absolutely no idea how to be a good spouse or parent.

It is interesting that we spend eleven years at school, and then maybe go on to further education to prepare for a career which may last thirty years. But we have little or no training for marriage or parenthood, which lasts a lifetime. Yet somehow, we expect that we should know what to do, even though no one has ever taught us. This is why strong, thorough marriage preparation is essential for engaged couples.

But our support must not stop there. When those couples have children, or as young families come in to the church, we can be pro-active in helping them meet the demands of parenthood. Many churches have woken up to this responsibility and opportunity, and offer a range of support ministries – Parent and Toddler groups, play groups, courses in parenting, practical support in terms of babysitting, etc. The possibilities are limited only by our creativity.

What about support/discussion groups for mums and dads; linking single-parent families with a mature couple in the church who can provide additional role modelling for the children, and practical support for the lone parent; older people in the church 'adopting' young families with no grandparents nearby; or families 'adopting' an older person whose children live far away? The needs in every community vary. Each church must discover the ways it can best support the families in its care.

Spiritual support

A church that has a strong teaching programme for the under fives is not only enriching the growth of those children, but is also ministering to their parents. This happens in two ways.

Firstly, on Sundays, if parents know that their children are loved, taught, and well looked after, they themselves are far more able to enter into worship. If they know their children are happy, they find it easier to give themselves to God in worship, and to hear from him about their own lives. For some parents, Sunday mornings are a lifeline, an oasis of peace in a chaotic week. Many mums with young children find that time alone with God (or alone at all!) is precious and rare. So when we are teaching their children we are ministering to them as well. (This assumes that the children are in a different venue than the adults – this issue is addressed in more detail in following sections.)

The second way we can support the parents is by encouragement and availability. Having worked with all the age groups under five, I have found that many parents are greatly helped and encouraged to know that someone else is interested in their children. A warm, personal greeting for each child as they enter the room assures the parents that I have noticed their child and am glad to see them. A brief comment at the door as the child is collected shows that I am aware of what activity they most enjoyed that morning, or of how they are making progress in certain areas.

To the parent of a baby who was left crying at the beginning, it is reassuring to say, 'Lauren settled down after only a few minutes and she really enjoyed looking at a picture book with me this morning'. To a parent who is concerned that their child doesn't play well with others, it is encouraging for them to hear, 'David shared the puzzles nicely today, and he and Sarah helped each other with one of the more difficult ones'.

It is not always easy to find something positive to say, especially at the end of a fraught or difficult session. Knowing that we want to encourage parents at the end may help us to look for positive things during the session. If there is not a specific comment you want to make to a parent, you may just want to tell them what their child was involved in. It is good to make the most of those few seconds on a Sunday in terms of encouragement.

Sometimes we may sense that a parent is particularly concerned or anxious about something, and then we can support by availability. We can ring them during the week to chat, or say at the time, 'We can't easily talk right now, but would you like to come round for a coffee one day this week?' For teachers who are at work during the week, this may not be possible. They may be able to mention sensitively their concern to another teacher who may be able to follow it up, or to the appropriate house group leader, or someone with responsibility for pastoral care.

Most parents are thrilled to know that they are not alone in the spiritual nurture of their children. Many parents are not sure how to teach their children about God, and will be helped by seeing what is done at church. If parents are very interested, they might even like to receive a note each month, giving Bible stories and themes so they can follow up at home. Teaching is not only good for the children, it provides spiritual support for their parents as well.

Happy families?

A generation ago, those who worked with children in the church could talk fairly safely and easily about the family in terms of father, mother and children, living in the same house. Today, this is not the case.

With the breakdown of marriage and family life in late twentieth century Western society, there is no longer a common definition of family. In many schools there are more children living in single-parent homes than children who live with both parents. In the church, as we reach out to the community, we have people from every imaginable family situation. How does this affect our work with under fives?

We need to be sensitive to the children we teach in two main areas; knowledge of their individual situations, and teaching about families.

It is important that we know relevant facts about the home situations of the children we minister to. This will help us in conversation with them, but in also knowing their needs and concerns. If we know that a child lives with just one parent, with grandparents, or in a foster home, our conversations with them will be more sensitive. A child may feel more secure when he realizes that his teacher knows about him and his family, whoever they may be.

Some of the children we teach may well come from homes where there is great unhappiness. They may frequently see or hear adults arguing and shouting. They may themselves be the victims of severe criticism, neglect, or physical or sexual abuse. If we suspect the latter, it may be necessary for us to notify the appropriate authorities. In some situations where we fear there is verbal and emotional abuse, we may be able to talk to a church leader for advice on how to help.

In some difficult family situations there is little we can

do because our help is not wanted. Anything we say may be seen as meddling. We can best help these children by asking God to enable us to understand their special needs, and in the brief time we have with them, to make a difference.

Anger, aggression, excessive crying, temper tantrums and clinginess can be symptoms of unhappiness at home. (On the other hand, we must not be overly suspicious – they can also be symptoms of tiredness, feeling unwell, or simply being in a bad mood!) If a child is exhibiting such things, we may want gently to find out what is happening at home. For children in families who are a committed part of the church, we may well already know if there are difficulties. For children who come from 'outside' the church, this information may not be so easy to obtain. Sometimes a casual visit to the home allows a teacher to see the child in his own environment, and may give clues to his behaviour at church.

As we work with children who struggle in one way or another at home, we need extra love and compassion combined with godly wisdom. Knowing about their home situations enables us to pray more intelligently for them, and helps us as we talk with them and teach them.

The other area in which we must be sensitive is teaching about family life. As a people committed to the word of God, we must somehow hold high God's ideal of one man and one woman for life, of sexual morality and purity, and of homes where children are loved, disciplined and nurtured. At the same time, we must help people to know God's love for them as individuals, to accept his forgiveness for their mistakes, and to receive his help to live with the consequences of their actions. Achieving this balance is somewhat akin to walking a tightrope!

In working with under fives, one of the areas we teach about is families. We want to help children understand that families are God's idea, that they love and care for us, and that we can be helping members of our families. This is not always easy, especially with children whose families are unhappy for various reasons. They may think that God's idea about families isn't a very good one!

If we are aware that there are children in our class who come from difficult situations, we must use great care when we talk about families. In one-to-one conversation with a child, we may be able to allow him to vent some of his anger and churned up feelings. In group time, this could be very damaging – both to the child himself, and the other children present.

Working with children from disrupted family situations is a challenge. Each child's needs are unique, and our approach must fit his personality as well as his level of understanding. As teachers of under fives we need the power and insight of the Holy Spirit to demonstrate the love of God to every child, whatever the make-up of his family. I believe that there are times when what we do with such children, even though our time is very limited, can be the thing that makes a difference.

It must break God's heart when he sees his plan for families so disfigured, almost unrecognizable, in our society. As his church, we must not only love people where they are, but we must call them back to the teaching of the Bible. For our generation, it is already too late. But as we properly love and teach the next generation, we can see God's kingdom come in terms of family life.

Evangelism

Most of what we have said in this section also applies to non-Christian parents. Although they may not be overtly interested in the spiritual welfare of their children, they would certainly share the struggles and concerns in every other area.

This provides the church with excellent opportunities for evangelism. Many adults will not come to church for themselves, but they will come for their children. There is still some residual sympathy with Christian things in Britain. No doubt we have all heard parents say that they think it is a good idea for children to 'go to Sunday School'.

I once heard someone say, 'Well, I went to Sunday School as a child and it didn't do me any harm'.

Although this desire for their children to attend Sunday School is often quite patronizing, we can still use it as an opportunity for God to work in their lives. They may come to church for the wrong reasons, but at least they will hear the right message when they get there!

Many parents, of course, don't want to *bring* their children to church. They want to *send* them to church! This can prove to be a real dilemma for the church. What we teach them in an hour on Sunday mornings is often completely negated when they get home. Children are smarter than we think. If Mum and Dad send them to church, but don't go themselves, they all too easily get the message that what they were told at church is not really important. There is no easy solution to the problem of unaccompanied children in church. Each church must decide how best to handle it.

In my own church we had the opportunity to rethink this issue some years ago, and came up with a policy that suits our situation. About eight years ago we moved from our church building to a school in order to have more space. With all the classrooms that were then available to us, we were able to start an all-age Christian education programme. I took on the responsibility of the under fives. We start with about half an hour of all-age worship, and then everyone goes to their teaching time. This set-up makes it difficult for children under five to be sent to church alone, because they need supervising in the worship time. Rather than having all the children sitting together, parents sit with their own children. So I am able to say to parents of under fives who want their children to come to 'Sunday School', that they are most welcome to bring them. After the worship time, they can go to the adult teaching while their child goes to class. Unfortunately, most people decide that is too great a price to pay. I am sad about this, but I believe that it is right for us to say that if it is important for children to go to church, it is important for their parents as well.

Apart from my belief that families should be in church together, I operate this policy from a safety point of view. I am not happy to have children under five on the premises without their parent or parents. Most people completely understand this and appreciate the fact that we take things seriously. This policy is more difficult with older children, and not really appropriate with teenagers. Each age group must handle things the way they think best.

The goal, then, is to develop such a good teaching programme for the under fives that it draws non-Christian parents to the church for the sake of their children. This is a brilliant vision, and I keep it ever in mind. The reality is, though, that Sunday church attendance is too threatening as the point of first contact for most people. We have to use other ways of reaching them.

This is where toddler groups, discussion groups and parenting classes are useful as a means of evangelism. Once we have made contact with people and shown them that we are aware of their needs and concerns as parents, then we can invite them to church. When non-Christians come to church and find that they and their children are welcomed and loved, they are far more likely to return. That is how a teaching programme for under fives can aid evangelism.

We have established that, although the home is the primary venue for passing on the faith, the church has a responsibility to support parents in this and other aspects of bringing up their children. We have also seen how the church can use under fives work to support evangelism. So we're becoming convinced that the church should be doing more than just tolerating or babysitting its youngest members. But how do we convince the church about that?

Chapter 4

Sharing the vision

I was walking along in front of the shops when I spotted someone from the church coming in the opposite direction. Fortunately, the path was fairly crowded, and I suddenly busied myself with rummaging through my handbag so as not to catch this person's eye. I wasn't trying to be antisocial, but I knew this particular person well enough to know that if we got started in conversation, I would be running late all morning! I didn't have the time nor the desire to be treated to a ten-minute discourse on this person's pet subject.

Have you ever known anyone like that in your church? They are often very nice, quite normal people. But when they get a commitment to a particular issue, they suddenly become so single minded that they drive everyone crazy! No matter what the topic of discussion, they somehow manage to link it to their specific concern.

As this person passed by without noticing me and I saw that it was safe to move on, I found myself wondering how often people avoid me in the street?! Most folk in our church know that I am strongly committed to teaching under fives. Do they turn around and walk the other way because they are afraid I might 'nab' them to teach? Have I actually diminished my chances of enthusing people about this important subject because I go on and on about it? I hope not.

Sometimes God shows us what he could accomplish through a certain area of ministry in our church. Sometimes he gives us a burden for a particular group of people, and a vision for what the church could be doing. Suddenly, we have the tendency to be transformed from humble, easy-to-work-with members of the body, into fanatical nag-bags! When people see us coming, they say, 'Oh no, not them again!' Why is it that we find it so hard to share effectively this issue about which we are so passionate?

There may be a number of explanations for this. In our favour, there is the excuse of over-exuberant zeal. We are so excited about our vision, that we can't stop talking about it. The problem with this is that when others do not find our enthusiasm 'catching', we may tend to find pride creeping in. We can't understand why people wouldn't want to be as excited as we are, so we conclude that there must be something wrong with them. Rather than wanting others to joyfully share our vision, we develop a 'them and us' stance, which sees 'us' as the spiritual ones, and 'them' as hindrances to what God wants to do. In fact, *we* may be largely to blame for not communicating lovingly, gently and wisely what we think God is saying to us or our church.

On the other hand, there are occasions when, despite doing everything right, the rest of the church or the leaders resist what we have to say. They seem to feel that any suggestion we make is a personal attack on their ministry or the church's life.

Most of the time failure to see vision become reality is a combination of these factors. So, what can we do about it? If I could come up with a foolproof formula for enabling a church to grasp a vision, then put that vision into practice, I would no doubt make many friends. I might even be able to write a bestseller!

Sadly, formulas that have to do with people are never foolproof. But principles are both reliable and adaptable. In this section we will look at some general principles for communicating vision, using teaching the under fives as the example.

Know your stuff

Before we make any attempt to persuade others about the need to teach the under fives, we must have a clear idea of what we are talking about. Admittedly, not a lot has been produced on this subject in Britain, but you will find at the end of this book a list of reading material you may find helpful. Also, a look at what other churches are doing in the area of under fives work might prove useful.

Many of us have the tendency to see what we think is a good idea and rush headlong into trying to put it into practice without thinking if and how it would work in our particular setting. So when you have finished reading this book, take some time to think and pray about what it has to say for your church situation. Make some notes of your impressions and ideas before you go to your church leaders. It is not necessary to have worked out the details of who, when and where, but it is important to be fairly clear about just what it is we are suggesting.

Start with the right person

Once you are reasonably confident about your vision and proposal of action, think carefully about who you should speak to first. Sometimes it may be appropriate to go straight to a church leader. Other times it may be better to 'test' your ideas with a trusted friend or another mature member of the church whose wisdom you value. It is not necessarily best to choose someone who you think will have sympathy with what you say. It may be a more accurate measure of the rightness of the vision to go to someone who has nothing to do with and little knowledge of under fives.

At this point it would certainly not be helpful to go around 'recruiting' a group of people to share your bias, and then go to the leaders and say, 'There are a lot of people who feel the same way I do'. That is sure to put them on the defensive before you even start! Ask God to guide you about who you should share with first.

Choose your moment

When you feel you are ready to talk to a church leader, be very careful about choosing the right time. Many a good idea in the church has never been put into practice because it was suggested at the wrong time in the wrong place. As you leave church on Sunday morning, you shake hands with your minister who has just preached his heart out, and there are fifty-seven people behind you queuing to get out of the door. This is probably not the best time to say,

'Let me tell you about this idea I've had. It's something our church really ought to be doing!'

Your minister would be far more affirmed and encouraged if you say to him, 'I've been thinking and praying about something lately, and I would be interested in what you have to say about it. When would be a good time for me to come and see you? Can I give you a ring to make an appointment?' If you know your pastor is in the middle of dealing with some fairly heavy counselling crisis or is under a great deal of pressure, it might be better to wait a few weeks before approaching him. If the idea is right, it is worth waiting for the right time. In the context of friendships, marriage, and the church, I am learning that it is not only *what* you say, but *when* you say it that makes a difference.

Work from principle to practice

This is a very good rule of thumb whenever you are trying to effect change – at home, at work or in the church. If I barge in with a list of things we need to be doing that involve a change from the present situation I am unlikely to find wholehearted support for my ideas. If, however, I present some principles, and people become convinced about them, they will find a way to work them out in practice.

If we approach an issue at the practical level, without any underlying commitment, people will always find a reason why we can't do it – we don't have the time, the money, the facilities, the manpower and so on. But if we change the way people view something in principle, then they will do all they can to put that principle into practice.

We can see this in every aspect of life. My girls, Bethany and Cara, are now old enough to make their own beds, tidy up the playroom, help with setting and clearing the table at mealtimes, and other jobs around the house. The frequency with which they do these things leaves something to be desired, however. I have realized recently that this is largely my fault. Although at times I am consistent in requiring them to help, I often just do the work myself rather than listening to their complaints about it. I have approached it at the practical level, rather than as a principle. In practice, very few children are keen to tidy up, make beds and so on. Not many adults are that thrilled about this either! But the principle is that we have a large house, there is a lot of work to be done, and it is right for each family member to help in the ways that they can. Often, we must do things because they are right, not because we feel like it. Hmm, perhaps I need to have a talk with my girls and help them to understand some principles . . .

The same thing happens in many work situations all the time. The boss comes in with a memo about new practices for his employees, and they moan and complain about the extra work it will make for them. If the boss had taken the time to explain why the new measures were more effective than the old ones, he might have found his workers more keen to comply. They might even have come up with a few good ideas of their own!

This scene is repeated in the church more often than I care to mention. Many good and helpful ideas never get off the ground because people concentrate on putting the practical structure into place before they have persuaded others of the principles involved. It is not necessary to convince the whole church before you can start anything new or make changes, but it is important to secure the commitment of key people who will support the venture.

These four steps are by no means exhaustive, nor are they guaranteed to work every time. But perhaps they will prove to be a start in helping you to share your vision.

A model for practice

Although the Bible gives us principles which must apply to every church, the way we carry out these principles will differ according to our situation. It would be wrong to imply that there is only one good way to work with under fives in the church. Not only that, it would be very foolish. Churches vary so widely in terms of physical facilities, size, distribution of age groups, and styles of worship that it would be impossible for every church to do things the same way.

Obviously, I am very much in favour of the model we operate in our church. But I am not naive enough, nor arrogant enough to believe that it will appeal to everyone, or even be the best for every church. It might be helpful, though, if I explain our practice so that I can say how it is a reflection of some principles I am committed to.

I mentioned earlier that for a number of years we have met in a school. This gives us some advantages that we didn't have in our small church premises. The main one is that we have as many classrooms as we need, and can therefore provide teaching in very specific age groups. We are a large church, averaging between fifty and sixty children under the age of five every Sunday. With this number it is necessary to divide them up into manageable groups. We have five classes. Before you switch off, thinking that your church only has fifty to sixty total attendance, please understand that if principles are right they can be adapted for any situation!

We start by meeting together for half an hour of worship, with the whole church family present. (Before I get caught out for not being completely accurate I should say that we do provide the class for the very youngest babies even during the first half-hour. This is not because we do not want them in worship. Many of them are actually asleep, and are therefore better left. Also, we find that most parents with infants not yet able to sit up prefer not to bring them into the large, crowded, and not particularly quiet gathering. They are perfectly free to, but most choose to take them to their class from the beginning.)

This is a time for the church family to enjoy being the people of God together, and to bring our worship to him. It is not a time for teaching and we do not have a children's 'spot'. Instead, we follow simple themes, use as few words as possible, and try to explain things in language that even a three- or four-year-old can understand. (They may not understand the concept, but they will understand most of the words we use.) This does not mean that the adults feel 'talked down to'. In fact, it often has the effect of enabling them to see things in a very practical way because we have explained them without using jargon or clichés. How to have an effective family worship time is the subject for a book itself, so we will not deal with it here.

At the end of the half-hour, everyone has their teaching time. Children under sixteen years are taught in classes according to age groups, and all those over sixteen years are taught together in a time of Biblical exposition. The teaching time lasts an hour. At the end of the time, parents collect their children.

How is this model an outworking of principles? Firstly, I am very committed to a time of family worship. By that I mean the church family, all ages learning to worship God together. I know this is not easy, but I believe it is very important as an expression of the whole body of Christ, male and female, young and old, married and single, black and white. I also believe that it is important for young children to see adults worshipping God so that they can learn how. Adults need to see that children are able to worship as well. All-age worship is a visual demonstration of much of what the Bible says − that we are all one in Christ, that all are accepted, that there are no barriers to those who are in Christ. It is worth persevering and working at (and it is hard work!) because of what it says to the church and to the community.

Although I am committed to the principle of all-age worship, I also believe that there is value in each person being taught the Bible in a way that is appropriate and relevant for their age and level of understanding. If we always meet together as the family, the adults do not have an opportunity to hear in-depth Bible teaching because the sermon has to be limited to ten minutes or so. The teenagers do not get the chance to see how the Bible has something specific to say to their situation, and the children (especially the youngest) are not able to have the Bible explained to them in ways that they can understand and put into practice. Although adults and teenagers may well have house groups in which to receive further Bible teaching, it is difficult to provide this opportunity for younger children other than on Sunday. Also, most house group study is discussion based. Sunday teaching provides the opportunity for exposition from someone who has had time to study in greater depth than is possible for most house group leaders.

Many churches operate on a similar principle by having everyone in for some of the service, then the children leave for their classes while the adults carry on the service. This can work very well as long as the children are not made to feel that they are simply being tolerated for as short a time as possible. They are then dismissed as all the adults breathe a sigh of relief (except for those who have drawn the short straw of having to go out with the children!) and get on with the really important part of the service. Of course I am exaggerating but you will understand that a lot is conveyed by our attitude. The teaching time, whether it be in classes or in the form of a sermon, is equally important for adults and children.

Two brief points which may be helpful in your thinking: firstly, is it possible to provide tapes of the adult teaching time for those who are teaching the children? This enables them to receive the same input, even though they haven't heard it live.

Secondly, many churches would find it impossible to have teaching in separate age groups because of a lack of space. Some have solved this dilemma by using the nearby homes of church members for older children's and teenage groups. Others have been able to find additional space by hiring nearby schools or halls. This brings difficulties such as transporting equipment, but most obstacles can be overcome if we are committed to making something work. Most of us do not have the luxury of purpose-built premises, so we have to be creative with what we have.

Chapter 5
Recruitment

Part of the theoretical base for teaching the under fives involves 'recruiting' teachers. It has been said that if you have the right teacher everything else will turn out right. If you have the wrong teacher, nothing else matters. This is an important principle to establish early on. It is a healthy antidote to an attitude which seems far too prevalent in many churches. Although no one would come right out and say it, there often seems to be an unspoken hierarchy of ministries. Work among adults may be seen as most important, followed by youth work, then children's work, and lastly, the 'crèche'. Many churches take care to find the right people for the right jobs in the areas they deem to be important, but just anybody can 'help out' with the under fives or youth or children's work. I am indebted to my husband for so accurately caricaturing this view. In *How to Close Your Church in a Decade*, he cites this example of a notice given out in a church:

> Please will someone volunteer to help out with the under fives; Mrs. Smith had nine children on her own last Sunday . . . and they all cried at the same time. It's *only* an hour a week and you don't need to be *any* good with children, just willing to be there. If three or four volunteered, then you could have a rota — so you would only have to do it once a month![1]

This notice could win the prize for 'How to devalue a whole segment of the church in one swift move'! We have already considered the importance of developing a biblical attitude

---

[1] Cohen, David and Stephen Gaukroger, *How to close your church in a decade.* (Scripture Union, 1992), p. 131.

towards young children. A church demonstrates the value it places on them by the regard in which it holds their teachers and the way it goes about choosing them.

Who should be a teacher?

What kind of person should be teaching the under fives? It goes without saying that the most important requirement is that every teacher be a committed Christian. How can we possibly communicate the love of Jesus if we do not know it for ourselves? Even very young children can sense the difference between someone who is committed to what they are doing and someone who is not.

Another issue which I would see as significant for those who are teaching every week is church membership. All the ministries of the church need to come under the authority of the leaders. People who are church members have shown their willingness to put themselves under that authority. They have also practically demonstrated their desire to be committed to that particular church family. Some churches that have a more informal view of membership may not feel so strongly about this matter.

In general, age is not a factor in teaching under fives – some of the best teachers have been grandparents! It is, of course, necessary that the person is fit and agile enough to be up and down off the floor, and able to lift young children.

Teaching pre-school age children is open to both men and women. Traditionally, it has been the domain of women, but there are a number of reasons why it is good to have male teachers as well:

- Some children respond better to men
- It is good for children to see men teaching about God
- Some children are in homes where there is no male role model and it is helpful for them to have a man to whom they can relate in a Christian context
- It helps other adults to see that passing on the faith to the children is not just a woman's responsibility.

And, of course, there is the fact that teaching the under fives is the way that God has gifted some men. It is the way they can most effectively contribute to the life of the church – not only by ministering to the children, but to their parents, as well.

Many people feel that they need to have had some experience of working with young children in order to teach them. This is not necessarily so. I have known some single people with no previous experience of children to be excellent teachers. As long as a person is willing to learn, prior experience is not necessary.

Another common assumption is that the best people to teach are those who are trained teachers, nursery nurses, etc. Again, this is not necessarily the case. In fact, many people who spend their week with children at work do not wish to spend Sunday with them as well. Often, people who do not have daily contact with children bring a real freshness to the time on Sunday.

There are a few groups of people who, for practical reasons, I prefer not to use as teachers on a weekly basis.

Young teenagers

The church is not legally bound by Social Services regulations unless they are looking after children for more

Yes, Pastor, I realise the class is half over by the time I get there, but remember, they need time to express themselves without the influence of adults.

than two hours consecutively. Even so, it seems good general practice not to use people under eighteen as leaders of a class. Many teenagers who have made clear commitments to Christ are wanting to become involved in some way. Perhaps they could be used as additional teachers once a month or so. This enables them to fulfil a meaningful role without depriving them of the teaching they would get in their own age group. At this pivotal stage in their lives they need to be the recipients of teaching ministry, not the givers of teaching.

Parents

In general, I try not to use the parents of under fives as teachers. Many church 'crèches' are organized on a rota basis, with the parents taking it in turns to look after the children. The task of nurturing the youngest members of the church family when they are at church, rather than at home, does not necessarily belong to the parents, but to those whom God has gifted to teach them in the church setting. Having looked at teaching the under fives as ministry to the *parents* as well as the children, it seems appropriate that they be free on Sundays to receive in worship, or contribute in some other way.

Another practical reason for not using parents every week is that because of their responsibilities at home they are often unable to get to church in the evenings or midweek. This makes Sunday morning all the more vital for them in terms of worship, teaching and contact with other adults.

Sometimes the people God has gifted to teach under fives do happen to be parents of young children. If they are wanting to be involved in weekly teaching, we try to make sure that they are able to get out at least two out of three Sunday evenings, and often midweek. This may happen by others in the church looking after their children sometimes on a Sunday night. Some young families in our church link up with another young family on Sunday evenings and the adults take it in turns to look after the children at one house or the other. This enables each adult to get out to the service more often than would otherwise be possible.

New Christians

The last group I would hesitate to use are new Christians. We are often guilty in the church of using the keenness and enthusiasm of new Christians in place of maturity. We can do them a real disservice by giving them too much responsibility too soon, especially when it requires them to miss the teaching and worship which they need in order to grow. Many people today are converted as adults, with no church background. They need time to get to know the Bible themselves before they try to teach it to others.

It is important for new Christians to realize early on that God wants them to be a contributing member of his body. They, along with teenagers and parents of young children may be able to be used less frequently than every week. Teaching once a month, perhaps, would enable them to make a valuable contribution without carrying too overwhelming a responsibility. It also provides an opportunity to identify those who may have a gift for teaching that can be developed in the future.

(For more information about using people on this rota basis, see 'Regulars or rotas?')

Enlisting teachers

Once you have determined the kind of people to look for as teachers, you must work out how many you need. Obviously, the younger the children, the higher the number of adults needed per child. For instance, in a group of three- to five-year-olds, a ratio of one adult to six or seven children may be fine. In a group of babies, this is not fine! Not unless all the babies are asleep and can be programmed only to wake up one at a time!

In a church with a large number of under fives, they will be divided into fairly narrow age bands. In fact, in some very big churches in America the children are not divided by year of birth, but by month of birth!

In a church with only a few children under five it is still

possible to provide meaningful teaching. Three or four children in one room, ranging in age from birth to five, presents a challenge, but good teaching is certainly attainable. This goes back to the issue of principle – if it is right, it can be adapted to any situation, no matter how large or small.

When you have decided if or how to divide the children into classes, and how many teachers you need, you can begin to enlist them. Look around the church, read through the membership list and ask God to show you the right people. Remember, the best people are not always the most obvious.

When you have someone in mind, you can either speak to them directly, or write a note. I often find that a note is best for two reasons: firstly, if the person is not expecting me to approach them and they have never worked with under fives before, they are more likely to think it through carefully if they have the time and privacy to do so. If I speak to them directly, they may be so surprised that they answer without really thinking clearly. Writing a note allows people to get over the shock in private, then think and pray about how to respond.

Secondly, a note is less threatening than having someone look you in the eye. It gives people more freedom to say no if they don't think it is right for them. I don't ever want someone to say yes to teaching under fives just because I am standing in front of them and they feel embarrassed to say no.

It is probably best to give only a small amount of information at first. Give the person time to think about it and get back to you. I usually end a note with something like this:

> *If you feel that this might be an area in which God can use you, please give me a ring and we'll arrange a time to talk so I can give you more details. If you don't think this is right for you, feel absolutely free to say so. Either way, I would appreciate it if you could get back to me as soon as possible.*

Asking someone to come and talk with you is not asking them to say yes. It is only saying that they are interested enough to know more details. The same principle applies whether you are writing a note or speaking to someone. Start with basic information and give people a few days to think about it. In most cases, a few days is enough time. If it is what God wants them to do, he can just as easily let them know in three or four days as in three or four weeks!

One thing I always assure people of is that I am not asking them to commit themselves forever. Many people are reluctant to say yes to anything in the church for fear of being saddled with it for the next twenty years! I ask people to try for three months, saying that if they don't feel it is working, or if *I* don't feel it is working, then we will say so. Most people won't know if this is their gift because so few churches have done it. People have never considered it because they've never had reason to. One of the best ways to find out if teaching the under fives is your gift is to try it! Not casually, or half-heartedly, but a serious attempt for a few months usually makes it clear.

Regulars or rotas?

Is it better to have the same teachers every week or can we use a rota? The answer is yes. It is possible to do both. The system that works most effectively will vary from church to church. In situations where only a few teachers are needed, it may be possible for the same people to teach every week. In churches that find staffing a problem, it may be better to find two people to 'job-share'. As long as they coordinate with one another to provide continuity in style and content, this can work.

In a setting like ours, which requires a large number of teachers, a combination of regulars and rotas meets the need. The two- to three-year class is fairly large and requires three teachers. Two teachers are committed to teaching every week. In addition there is a rota of four people who each help once every four weeks. Having two regular teachers provides continuity and familiarity for the children. Because the rota people are there only once a month they bring variety and freshness. With only four people on a rota, the children soon get to know them all.

In our youngest group, which is birth until a baby is crawling, two people share the job, along with four people on a rota. The parents know that either Ruth or Jane will be there every week, so it gives them confidence, and enables Jane and Ruth to know the babies well. The people doing one class every four weeks are also able to keep fairly up to date with the babies' different personalities and schedules.

No system is perfect. The security of the same teacher each week is important for children. On the other hand, it is also stimulating for them to be involved with a variety of adults. Sometimes trial and error is the only way to find out what is workable in a specific situation. We may think that the ideal is the same teachers every week. In reality, that may not be possible. We must assess our own situation and decide how we can best meet the needs, given the children and teachers we have.

Is teaching a life sentence?

Have you ever seen the bumper sticker that says, 'A dog isn't just for Christmas . . . it's for life'? Many people feel that way about taking on responsibility in the church, particularly teaching in Christian education. They fear that if they say yes, they will be doing it forever. All too often this has been true! Too many people have said, 'I went in as a relief teacher at sixteen, and I was still doing it at sixty-five!'

Giving people a rest from their responsibilities is not only practical, it is biblical. In the Old Testament, the ground was to lay fallow every seventh year – even the soil had a sabbath! The gospels often record that Jesus was resting, or retreating from the crowds in order to spend time with God. If Jesus needed time away from the normal activities of life, then how much more does this principle apply to us? We never have a break from our responsibility to live and grow as Christians, but sometimes we need a rest from certain aspects of our activity in the church.

For me, part of the development of the under fives programme involves building up a pool of teachers, so that each teacher can have a break of about six months every two to three years. At the end of the six months, some return to teaching, some do not. This break is particularly valuable in situations where teachers of children are not part of the adult teaching time. When people have had six months to receive that ministry and to be free of the responsibility of weekly planning and preparation, they return to teaching refreshed and with new enthusiasm.

There are times, of course, when this does not work out quite so simply, but it seems good general practice. When I approach people about teaching in the first place, they find it easier to say yes when they know that they are allowed a break! Also, there are some people who are able to teach during someone's six months off, but would find a longer stint too demanding.

No matter how committed we may feel to teaching the under fives, we all need a break sometimes. A 'sabbatical' gives us breathing space, practically and spiritually. If God is calling us to a different ministry, we are then free to do that. If he wants us to stay where we are, then that call will be confirmed.

Teaching the under fives should be viewed as a joy and a privilege, not a life sentence! Although arranging for people to have a rest from teaching is not always easy to organize, it is an important part of helping teachers to stay fresh and maintain the right perspective.

Chapter 6
Child development

We have looked at why we should teach the under fives, at supporting parents and families, and at the church's attitude to young children. We have also discussed what kinds of people we are looking for as teachers and how we share our vision for working with pre-school age children. Before we can discuss what and how to teach the under fives we need to understand their development. In this section, we will take a brief 'tour' of child development.

Studies of human development do not focus only on the physical stages that people move through, but also on the mental and emotional aspects of life. It is important to see how these change and develop alongside one another. Looking at mental progress in isolation from physical and emotional growth does not enable us to see the individual as a whole person. We need to look at development in all areas of life – physical, mental, emotional/social and moral/spiritual.

Many textbooks have been written about child development. Most bookstores stock books aimed at new parents that help them to know what to expect of their child at various stages. This section is by no means an in-depth study, so you may find that reading some of these more detailed books is helpful. Although we shall look at all four areas of development, we will concentrate more on the emotional and spiritual aspects than many secular books do.

Each child is unique, created and loved by God. No two children will ever be exactly the same. But all children go through the same basic stages of development. The *order* in which they master tasks is generally the same, but the *rate* at which they master them differs for each child.

A study of these tasks is meant to be a guideline,

enabling us to know what to expect, and in what order. It is not meant as a strait-jacket into which we put all children, constantly comparing them with others. This only causes unnecessary worry when one child is not like another. Obviously, if a child seems to be way outside the common pattern of things, it is worth observing them, and possibly referring them to a doctor or health visitor. But most children master all the developmental tasks within a few months of each other. It is the pattern, not the timing, that is important.

As teachers and as parents, understanding where a child is developmentally enables us to teach in relevant and effective ways. Knowing what they are capable of physically allows us to provide appropriate activities for learning. Knowing what they can understand at a mental and spiritual level helps us to teach the Bible meaningfully. And, of course, an awareness of their emotional and social progress means that we can better understand their behaviour and the way they relate to other children and adults.

So, let's start at the very beginning . . .

Before birth

In nine months a human foetus undergoes massive physical development – from one fertilized cell to a fully functioning body, capable of existing outside the protected environment of its mother's womb. But that is not the end of the story. Even before birth a baby can hear, respond to touch, and is affected by its mother's emotional state. When she is stressed, her body releases hormones that reach the baby through the placenta. The ability to hear (although the sounds are muffled by the fluid in the womb) explains why a baby responds to its mother's voice so soon after birth. The baby has been hearing it for several months!

Babies

Physical

Newborn babies are completely dependent on others. They cannot feed themselves, dress themselves or even reposition themselves. As mentioned earlier, in the early days of their lives, the only purposeful movement they are capable of is sucking — and that is a reflex action!

All this very quickly begins to change, however. Within a few weeks, their eyes will be able to focus on nearby objects. They may attempt to lift their heads to see something. You may notice a slight tightening of their muscles when they are lifted. At this stage, they may be sleeping as much as 21 out of 24 hours! This is normal — newborn babies have much growing to do, and it takes a lot of energy. Let them sleep as much as they want to! In the second month they will be awake for longer periods. Their eyes will follow an object from side to side.

By three months they will turn their heads to a familiar voice. They may also bat their hands at an object dangled in front of them. They may grasp things with their hands, but they are not able to purposefully let go. They can now lift their heads when lying on their stomachs.

At four months babies will reach for objects in front of them and will turn their heads to find the source of sound. Their head and neck muscles are stronger now, so you may not need to put your hand behind their heads when holding them. They will discover their fingers and become fascinated by them, although they will not realize they are part of their bodies. They will look at them, clasp them together and, of course, taste them. After this, everything starts going in their mouths. It becomes an instrument for learning and discovery.

By five months babies can hold a toy in both hands, or change a toy from one hand to another. They may start to roll over, and they can sit for short periods with support.

Somewhere around six to seven months they will be able to sit for a little while without support. They will also discover their feet. They are a nice toy and will also fit in their mouths.

At about nine months they can get on to their hands and knees and rock back and forth. They will learn to put a hand, then a knee forward, and soon they will be crawling. They may even be able to crawl up the stairs – but they won't be able to get down again. Not intentionally, anyway! Now that they can move, they can crawl to something they see or want (including things that are not toys!). They will probably enjoy standing with help. They can now use their first finger and thumb together to pick up an object.

By one year babies can pull themselves up to stand, or even be able to stand alone. Then they may cry because they don't know how to sit down again. Next, they 'walk' in a sidestep, holding on to the furniture. They also use their eyes and their hands more than their mouths for exploration. They may enjoy taking things apart or emptying containers of their contents, but they won't be able to put them back again.

Mental

At birth, babies do not really think, they only react. But very soon their behaviour begins to have purpose. Within a few weeks they will follow an object with their eyes. They become sight and sound 'hungry', searching for things to see and hear. They respond well to colours and movement. They are entertained by having something to listen to, like music, or people talking. (But they also need times of quiet!) At this stage, if something moves out of their sight, it ceases to exist – out of sight, out of mind.

Within a few months they begin to recognize the shape of things. If an object looks like a bottle, they know it means food. Familiar sounds can be comforting, too, like the sound of mother's voice. Even the sound of approaching footsteps is a signal that someone is coming.

At five months they may turn an object around to inspect

the other side of it. They think that objects in pictures are real, and may reach out for them or try to pick them up. When they discover their feet, they do not yet realize that they are attached to their body. Somewhere between five and eight months the difference between mother's face and the face of a stranger becomes significant. This can cause what is often referred to as 'stranger anxiety'.

Another major mental step is the discovery of cause and effect. When they accidentally drop something from their highchair, they watch. They see and hear it hit the floor. They learn that if they let go of something, it falls and makes a noise. This is a great discovery. They do it again. Also, if they drop it, someone will pick it up. To adults, this is an annoying game. To a baby it is a significant mental milestone. They have learned that they can cause things to happen.

Another major mental step is learning that things still exist even when they cannot see them. This may happen around eight or nine months. They may cry when you take things away. Before, they forgot about it once they couldn't see it. Now they remember.

At ten to twelve months when you hold them up to look in a mirror, they will recognize you, but not themselves. If you give them a book, they will put it in the right position for reading and turn pages, usually several at a time. Their memory is developing such that they may be able to remember the next day where they put the book. They enjoy stacking things, and taking apart nesting toys. They will be unable to put them back in the right order because they can't understand why the big beaker does not fit into the little one.

During the first year there is major mental development. Babies learn how to move in order to explore. This exploration is done through all the senses – seeing, hearing, tasting, touching and smelling.

Emotional/Social

In the first month of life a baby's emotions may seem very intense and changeable. They can be very content one minute and the next minute be crying loudly. Crying is the response for everything – hunger, pain or being uncomfortable. In the second month they may stop crying when someone holds them, or even talks to them.

From very early on babies respond to people talking to them. By six to eight weeks they are smiling, then even gurgling or wriggling when spoken to. They may soon make cooing sounds, trying to talk back. By about eight months they will be making sounds like 'da-da-da' or 'ma-ma-ma'. They are imitating what they hear. It is important to speak properly to a baby instead of using baby talk all the time. They learn to speak by listening to those around them.

By about six months they are responding to parental emotions. If mother speaks crossly, they may frown. If Dad laughs, they may smile. They also recognize their own name.

'Stranger anxiety' can seem like a social setback. It is actually evidence of an emotional attachment to their parents or carers.

At twelve months they will watch adults and often try to imitate. They can understand and obey a simple command like 'wave to Daddy' or 'give it to Mummy'. They will be able to give hugs and sloppy kisses. They will probably enjoy hearing rhymes and being sung to.

Moral/Spiritual

A child's moral and spiritual development begins at birth. The first year of life is crucial for the development of trust. If their needs are met consistently, babies learn that they can trust. If they are not met, or if they are left to cry for extended periods, they learn not to trust. They also learn not to express their needs because they sense that no one will meet them. Trust is an inherently spiritual quality. If children learn that they can trust the adults in their lives, they will form a strong foundation for trust in God. If, however, they cannot trust the adults they *can* see, how will they trust the God they cannot see?

Consistently meeting the physical needs of babies helps

them to feel secure, to know that they are loved. Their general view of themselves and of life is developed in this first year. When we use their names in positive and encouraging ways instead of just for correction or in anger, they are helped to feel worthwhile. When we meet their physical needs as well as their needs for affection, we help them to acquire a positive outlook. They will see life as pleasant rather than unpleasant.

By about four months babies can begin to learn patience, another spiritual quality. Because they know they can trust you to meet their needs, they can learn to wait. They know that you will feed them, so they learn to wait while they see you start to prepare their bottle or food. They know what comes next.

At about eight months they can begin to learn about sharing. They hold out a toy to Mum, she takes it, then gives it back in a moment. They may cry when she actually takes it away, but as she gives it back they are learning the first step of sharing – being able to let go of something, even just for a minute.

As they reach the age of 'stranger anxiety' they can be helped by not being left with complete strangers. This is why consistency in teachers at church is helpful. They are also now developing a memory. If they are left with someone different every week at church they will soon build up a store of unhappy memories about church.

It is also helpful to their development of trust that they *are* actually left. They learn that Mummy and Daddy leave them, but that they come back. Generally the solution to stranger anxiety is not to stop leaving them, but to leave them with a kiss and a 'see you soon'. They may be distressed, but they will learn that Mummy and Daddy do come back.

(N.B. I would not recommend that a parent stay with a child for a minute or two, then sneak away without the child noticing. This can appear underhanded to the child, and will teach him not to turn his back in case he gets left. This will not help him in developing trust.)

We mentioned that it is important to speak properly even to babies because it is by hearing words used that they begin to understand their meaning. When we say to a newborn baby, 'Mummy loves you', they do not know what that means. But as they hear those words frequently, spoken in a warm and gentle way and accompanied by loving and consistent meeting of their physical needs, they take on significance for them.

In the same way, we can aid their spiritual development from their first days by letting them hear the name of Jesus used often and lovingly. As they hear that God loves them, that God made them, that Jesus loves them, they will come to understand that those words are important.

Have you ever seen a father out with a young baby for a walk? The baby is observing everything around him, and suddenly becomes excited and points to something. Dad will almost automatically look in that direction then say, 'Oh yes. Look, there's a dog. That's a dog.' Even though the child cannot yet speak, his father is helping him develop the foundations for his later vocabulary. The technical name for this is 'labelling'. We tell children the name for many things which they see and hear.

As we introduce a baby to the things we see every day, so we can just as naturally introduce him to the things of God. As Dad talks to him about the dog he can also say, 'Thank you, God, for eyes to see the dog'. Children can begin to learn about the Bible as we say to them, 'I love you. Jesus loves you, too. The Bible says that Jesus loves us'. These are the kinds of things babies need to hear at home and at church. As they approach twelve months and their memory starts to function, they will remember the things we tell them, even though they cannot yet say them themselves.

I am quite sure that this natural way of helping our children to learn about God and to know him is part of the outworking of Deuteronomy chapter six, 'Impress them [these commands] on your children' (verse 7). The problem for most of us is that we don't find it easy to speak of the things of God to one another, let alone to our children. We say, 'We were really fortunate that it didn't rain for our picnic', instead of 'Thanks, Lord, for the sunshine'. We can pray, and ask God to help us become more comfortable with our words about him. Perhaps then our children will grow up without our inhibitions, and be those who delight to speak of the things of God.

The first year of life is vital for the foundation of spiritual development. As babies have their physical needs met consistently and lovingly, they learn trust. As they hear the names of God and Jesus used in positive, affectionate and reverent ways, they realize that they are important. As they hear their own name used with love and encouragement, they form a healthy view of themselves, knowing that they are loved and valued.

Toddlers

Physical

The most significant physical task of a toddler is learning to walk. This requires a great deal of concentration and energy. Once they have learned how, they will want to do it all the time! Soon they will be able to walk and carry something as well, then carry something in each hand. They will learn to come down the stairs, either by crawling down backwards, or by 'bumping' down on their bottoms.

Toddlers can use their hands for more detailed tasks now. They can stack a few bricks, and as they approach two they may be able to work simple puzzles. The things they took apart in their first year they may now be able to put together again. Towards two they can hold a chunky crayon and scribble, although they may well alternate using right and left hands.

By about fifteen months they can hold a cup by themselves, and may attempt to use a spoon for feeding. They will be able to take off some of their clothes (mostly at inconvenient times!), but not put them back on.

Mental

In this second year of life mental development is linked to physical experiences. Toddlers learn by what they do. Because of this, they want to do many things. To them, the world is for exploring, for finding out what things can and cannot do. They may be fascinated by switching something on and off. They are not interested in why it works, only that it does work.

They now have mental pictures of many of the words they know. So when you say, 'drink', they know what you mean. When you say, 'Here comes Daddy', they know who you mean. As they near age two they understand most of what you say to them.

Between the first and second year, their vocabulary may increase to as many as 100 words. This may not begin to happen until after they have mastered walking – it is difficult to do two things at once! They are learning how to use language to express themselves. They may say 'book' when they want you to read to them, or 'wet' when they need to have their nappy changed. They will start putting two words together and making animal noises. They can point to various parts of their body, or to different people when named.

Although they may move rapidly from one toy to another, their attention span begins to increase. They may play alone for longer periods of time.

Emotional/Social

As toddlers are learning to walk, they will have many bumps and falls. Falling doesn't hurt them nearly as much as it would hurt an adult – they don't have as far to go. Because they are not frightened they do not stiffen when they fall. They will not worry about these falls and bumps unless they see that those around them are worried. They will not be afraid to climb and explore unless they sense that those caring for them are afraid.

Toddlers will enjoy the company of an adult, and enjoy sharing experiences with them. They will not yet play with other children, although they may play alongside them. They may explore other children by patting, touching or poking at them. At this age, choice of toys is not determined by sex. Boys will happily play with dolls, girls with cars and trains. Any preference for gender-related toys is probably more to do with what we make available for them to play with.

This is the age for independence. They want to do everything by themselves. They will make clear what they want to do and what they don't want to do. There are times when we can let them do those things that they can do for themselves. It often requires a great deal of patience. It is important, though, for it balances the times that we cannot let them do things for themselves.

Although they will be exploring and discovering many new things, they will also need the security of some routine. Knowing that things have a place and that they can find them in their place may help. A room that is cluttered with too many toys can be frustrating for them. They can only make limited choices. Having only some of the toys out at any given time may be more appropriate. Now that they are able to put things back together they can begin to learn to tidy up one set of toys before getting out another.

Moral/Spiritual

Toddlers watch adults and imitate them. They will learn much about the way to treat other people by the way they see adults behaving. They need to see an example of kindness, respect and gentleness.

In learning to exert their independence, they will begin to make choices. When should they do what they are told instead of what they want? When should they keep on making a fuss to get what they want? What can they touch and not touch? What should they do when someone hits them? They need guidance to know what is appropriate behaviour. When they make a right choice, notice and encourage them. When they choose the wrong thing, tell them why, and what would be the better thing to do. 'I asked you not to touch the video. If you touch it in the wrong place it might get broken, then we would not be able to use it. You can play with your puzzle instead.' At this age, they are often not able to work out the consequences of their actions. They will not know unless they are told, that playing with the video could break it. They do not know which items are built to withstand their child-like explorations and which are not.

They may often try to assert their will. This is part of their moral development. They need to know that there are limits, and that the person caring for them is in control. Although they may be frustrated by this, it gives them security.

The constant motion associated with a toddler flows out of God-given curiosity. This desire to learn and explore must be nurtured and encouraged, but also guided. Obviously, we must protect children from danger and correct wrong behaviour. But if we set too many limits, if we are always saying 'no' and stopping them doing things, we may strangle their curiosity. They may feel it is wrong to do new things, and may become increasingly dependent. I have a friend who once told me that when her daughter came asking to do something, before she said 'no', she always asked herself, 'why not?'. Often we automatically say 'no' to what a child is doing, without a good reason why they shouldn't do it. The reason is sometimes that we can't be bothered to take the time to allow them to try something new or different.

Many toddlers spend their lives being told to hurry up or walk faster. They are not dawdling on purpose. There is so much to see and hear all around them. We may have seen it all before, but they haven't. Sometimes we are genuinely short of time, but often we can turn those moments into valuable spiritual input. As they gaze at all the fruits in the supermarket, we can take just a minute to say, 'Look at all the beautiful colours of fruit. I'm glad God gives us so many good things to eat.' Perhaps even we will be thrilled again with the great beauty and variety of God's good gifts to us!

Before children can learn to share, they have to understand what is theirs. At this age, if they are holding a toy or playing with it, they think it is theirs. They cannot understand that it may actually belong to someone else. Forcing them to 'share' when they do not understand about possession does not teach them to be generous. They perceive that you are making them do what they do not want to do. This is difficult, and needs to be handled gently and creatively, perhaps by offering alternative toys. When they do give a toy to another child you can thank them and encourage them. This will mean it is more likely to happen again.

The concept of sharing is outside the mental capabilities of young children. They are only just learning to see the world from their own point of view. They cannot yet see it from someone else's. When an adult asks or forces them to share their toy, it usually means that they have to give it up for someone else to play with. From their point of view this is grossly unfair. They only understand that *they* want to play with it. They cannot yet imagine that if they like it, another child might like it, too. Perhaps it is more realistic and helpful if we start by teaching them to take turns. They may play with it for a few minutes, then the other child can have a turn. In a few minutes it will be their turn again. Even this is not easy to teach. It requires patience and careful monitoring. Learning to take turns is the foundation for learning to share.

At twelve months children cannot understand about 'valuables'. They cannot appreciate that the video recorder costs more than all their toys combined. They have no idea that the china figurine on the fireplace has great sentimental value. Although they must begin to learn that there are things they cannot touch, too many 'no's can be overwhelming. Perhaps it is best to move the most valuable or breakable items out of reach until they are older.

In the second year of life children will want to please those to whom they have a strong attachment. In that way those people have power over them. With this power comes a responsibility to be consistent in standards of right and wrong, and to be an example that is good for them to imitate.

Two- and three-year-olds

Physical

The third year of life is one of transition from baby to child. This can be awkward physically (and in other ways, too!). The mastery of walking means that two-year-olds want to walk down as well as up stairs. This is harder than it looks. They can climb now, too. This means they can reach all kinds of things! Use caution with regard to medicines and cleaning solutions.

They can now feed themselves fairly well, and even make reasonable attempts at cleaning their own teeth. They can undo zips, poppers, and maybe even buttons, although they will not be able to do them up again.

Their dexterity increases greatly. Their drawing may become more purposeful as circular movements begin to replace scribbles. Colouring within lines is beyond their physical ability. Plain paper rather than colouring books will give them more freedom.

This year they will gain control over their bladder and bowels.

Mental

Vocabulary is constantly on the increase, and children now speak in sentences. Their brains often work faster than their mouths, so stuttering is not unusual. Grammar is a very difficult thing to learn, and this often results in statements like, 'I played with my toys and I goed to the park'. These things will sort themselves out. A child can best be helped by hearing adults speak clearly and correctly.

They are now learning about numbers and can count. That is, they can say the numbers in order. But they may not be able to correctly count how many bricks are in their tower.

They are learning about sizes, too, and may be able to say which is bigger or smaller. They begin to have some understanding of time in relation to activities, for example, we get dressed before we eat breakfast, we go to bed when it is night. They do not yet know how long five minutes is. It might as well be a week to them!

All their thinking is related to their experiences. They can only understand things concretely. They are not capable of abstract thought. They cannot think things through by reason, but only by how things look to them. If they pull down the window shade during the day, they may say, 'Look! I made it dark!' To them, pulling down the shade makes the sun go away.

Often we try to explain things to them with our ability to use logic and link abstract thoughts. We may get frustrated when they ask the same question again. We thought we gave a satisfactory answer, but we forget that they cannot think like we do, and they do not know all that we know.

Two-year-olds rarely know the answer to the question 'why?'. When they have grabbed a toy from another child and we ask, 'Why did you do that?', they are not able to answer. They genuinely do not know why. Even as adults we do not always know why we do the things we do. Rather than asking, 'Why did you do this?' or 'Why were you naughty?', it might be more helpful to identify the unacceptable behaviour and explain why it is so. For example: 'You took the ball away from Sarah. She wants to play with it now, so you must not take it away from her. That is not kind. You can play with the car now, and in a minute you can have a turn with the ball.' They may not be impressed with your explanation, but you have stopped the wrong behaviour and given them some words to help them understand. It is difficult to be consistent in this, but most children eventually begin to understand.

Emotional/Social

In *Understanding Today's Preschoolers*, an American book about under fives, the section on child development is written in the first person, from the child's point of view. This gives some very helpful insights:

> *I am wrongly referred to as 'terrible' just because I am negative (I say no often and emphatically) and am rebellious (I want my way). Actually, this can be viewed as a positive stage in my development. I am scaling a big hurdle in my development.*
>
> *I am not good at getting along with others. That's because I can't see things from their point of view. I mostly know what I want. I am just learning to take turns.*
>
> *. . . I can be abrupt in changing my mind. I want what I want now. I like to give orders. I insist that I dress myself, which I can't do: but I will violently resist if you try to help. When I decide I can't, I may strike out at you for not assisting me.*
>
> *My frequent change of moods may be frustrating for you. Just think what it is for me. I want, and I don't want. Making a decision is difficult for me. I am learning to have a mind and will of my own.*
>
> *. . . When I am exasperating, try to be patient and remember that I am discovering who I am and what you expect of me. On the one hand, I am trying to be big and gain self-control. You expect me to conform to many behaviours which you consider appropriate. A few months ago I didn't even know I was a person. To become a person in my own right, I sometimes disagree with or defy you. I am trying to establish my preferences. Sometimes you disagree with my preferences of behaviour. Do I do what my parents want me to do? Do I do what I want to do? It seems I can't do both at the same time.*
>
> *. . . If I am to rely on myself and feel capable of doing the tasks before me, I must be given the*

> *right to choose. I must also learn some limits. I get many commands. I have a difficult time learning rules. To remember a rule, I have to think about too many things at one time – when and where and under what conditions I can and cannot do.*
>
> *I know that you expect me to gain bowel and bladder control. How you assist me in this affects my feelings about myself and your power. Shaming me for an 'accident' is a way of using your power over someone smaller. Shaming me for what I cannot help or don't know how to do may cause me to be deceitful. I may even hide to do it. Shaming me causes me to doubt my worth. Accept my efforts to gain control, and I will feel worthwhile.*
>
> *. . . The way I get along with others and how I behave to get what I want are well established by age three. These patterns of behaviour are difficult to change.*[1]

In this passage the child mentions not being good at getting along with others because he can't see things from their point of view. This is often confused with selfishness. Young children are self-centred, as opposed to selfish. Selfish is when I can see someone else's point of view, but I choose mine anyway. I know how others feel or what they want, but I am more interested in me. Self-centred is viewing things from a limited perspective – my own!

Two-year-olds do not yet have the necessary mental processes to understand how another person feels. They cannot put themselves in their place. So when they are asked, 'How do you think Mark feels when you hit him?', they cannot answer because they honestly do not know. It hurts when someone hits them, but they do not realize

---

[1] Waldrop, C. Sybil, *Understanding Today's Preschoolers* (Convention Press, 1982), pp. 30–31.

that it must hurt others when they hit them. We must assist children in learning to see things from another's point of view. Rather than asking the above question, it might be more helpful to say, 'Please don't hit Mark. It hurts him when you do that and makes him sad'. As they get a bit older they can also be helped to understand if they are told, 'You do not like it if Mark hits you. He does not want you to hit him either'.

Young children are often accused of being selfish when they are actually only being self-centred. They are not choosing their own wishes above the wishes of others. They only know what they want and are not yet aware that others have preferences too.

The last paragraph of the quote concerns relationships with others. This is a crucial time for social development. At this age, patterns of relating to other people are becoming firmly established and will be difficult to alter. If children get what they want by throwing tantrums or by whining, they will learn to manipulate people to get their own way.

I well remember one of my own children telling me, 'If you don't let me do what I want I will be naughty and horrible'. I quickly assured her that this approach would not get her very far, and that she was more likely to get what she wanted by behaving nicely!

Children soon learn whether crying, making a scene or throwing a tantrum will get them what they want. If it does, they develop a pattern of controlling others by manipulation. We have already said that children are imitators of the adults in their lives. If they see us manipulating others to get what we want, they will learn to do the same. If, on the other hand, they see us treat them and others with respect, they will learn to respect the wants and needs of others.

Moral/Spiritual

The child is beginning to develop a conscience, not motivated by an internal conviction of right and wrong, but determined by external factors. What adults allow him to do is right, what they don't allow is wrong. Thus, consistency is important in this first stage of conscience development. If throwing bricks around is allowed one day and not allowed the next, they become confused. If hitting some people is okay but hitting others is not okay, they are unable to know which is which.

Important foundations are laid for forgiveness and unconditional love. It is not helpful for a young child to hear an adult say, 'I'm not talking to you because you were naughty', or, 'I won't give you a hug right now because you have been horrible'. They need to know that you always love them, even when you do not like what they are doing. Isn't it good that God doesn't stop talking to us just because we have been horrible!

Often children of this age say or do things which entertain and amuse others. 'Party pieces' are fun from time to time, but we need to be careful that children do not interpret that they are loved or accepted more when they 'perform'. As they become aware that you always love them, they can also begin to be aware that God always loves them.

In the third year children begin to understand the concept of family. They have an awe and wonder at creation. They will be able to know some things about Jesus; that he was born, that he grew up, that he was part of a family. They begin to understand that Jesus loves people and wants people to love and help each other.

Affirming their attempts to be kind or helpful will encourage a positive self-image. It will also encourage further attempts!

Three- and four-year-olds

Physical

Development of the larger muscles means that three-year-olds can jump, walk on their toes, use a climbing frame, throw a ball and ride a tricycle. At age four they can hop on one foot, skip, somersault and kick a ball with some accuracy.

Small muscles are developing, too. They may be able to draw a person now, or at least a head and face. As they approach four they may draw arms and legs as well, but probably no body! They will begin to use scissors, and can manage well with pencils and ordinary crayons as opposed to chunky ones. Four-year-olds may be able to write their own name, or at least form some of the letters.

At three they can usually manage by themselves in the toilet, although some dungarees and belts can be a bit tricky! As the months go by, four-year-olds will learn to dress themselves and put on their own shoes. You will still need to tie them for them. At this age velcro fastenings give a great deal of independence!

Mental

Vocabulary is ever on the increase and three-year-olds will talk freely, both to themselves and others. They can remember rhymes well now, and enjoy singing. They have many mental images associated with words or experiences. This enables them to pretend in play – either in role play or in pretending actions.

Three- and four-year-olds are very inquisitive. They are often asking why or how. This is their God-given curiosity at work again. Much patience is required to answer their questions in ways they can understand.

Four-year-olds are often highly imaginative. They may spin great tales of flight and fancy. Sometimes they find it difficult to distinguish fact from fantasy. They may genuinely believe the stories they hear about fairies and dragons. Thus, when a four-year-old tells you he has just seen a fairy queen in the back garden, he is not deliberately lying. He is trying to work out what is fantasy and what is reality.

At four children are still not able to think logically. They cannot combine several thoughts to reach a conclusion. They are literalists – they think concretely and cannot understand the abstract meaning of words. When they hear an adult saying, 'He is a barrel of laughs', they are wondering how you put laughs into a wooden container.

Sarcasm is beyond a young child as well. I remember when Samuel, my youngest child, spilled his drink at teatime. It went all over the table and dripped onto the floor. I said, 'Thanks a lot, Sam!' Cara, who was just five, said 'Mummy, why did you say thank you to Samuel? You didn't really want him to spill his drink did you?'

At this age, language exceeds thinking. That is, children can talk about things they do not understand. And talk they do! If no one happens to be around they will chatter on to themselves, using words they have heard without having any idea what they mean. They are not unlike some preachers: perfectly content to hear themselves talk whether they make sense or not!

This ability to remember and repeat things without understanding has serious implications with regard to spiritual things. We will look at this in more detail later, but for now it is sufficient to say that children are capable of memorizing large amounts of words, including Bible verses, without having any idea of what they are saying. We often think children understand more than they do because of their large vocabulary.

Emotional/Social

Three-year-olds are now ready to play with other children rather than alongside them. They are beginning to understand what belongs to whom, and may be able to take turns. Sharing is still very difficult. If children perceive that something is theirs, they will struggle to understand why they have to let someone else play with it.

They are able to discern emotion by facial expression and tone of voice. They know whether their parents are pleased or displeased with them or with a situation. At four they may start to express their own emotions – 'I am happy' or 'I feel sad'.

Four-year-olds imitate adults in actions and attitudes. They may be fascinated with the jobs they see adults doing, particularly if those jobs involve uniforms, such as firemen, nurses, postmen or train drivers. They may pretend to talk on the telephone or type. They may pretend to use a hammer and saw, or do the cooking. It is always interesting to watch children when they are imitating you. Many is the time Steve and I have observed our own children 'playing' church. One will announce the hymns and 'read' the Bible, and the other will preach the sermon! It is often very sobering to hear our children speaking to each other in the same way that we speak to them. They learn a lot, positively or negatively, from the way they see us treat them and others.

At four children can do many things for themselves. They can also begin to do things for other people. They can do things that are helpful at home. They can help look after a younger child. They can help another child with a difficult puzzle or toy. They are also developing a sense of humour and can have a real sense of fun with adults.

Moral/Spiritual

Three- or four-year-olds think that their parents, or any adults who have responsibility for them, are infallible. They will believe without question what they are told. The rules adults make are law to them. When one child sees another doing something he is not allowed to do he may say, 'You are not supposed to do that'. When asked why, he may say, 'Because my dad says so'. At this stage of their moral development children will obey the rules not from an inner desire to do the right thing, but in order to avoid punishment. Their moral behaviour is limited by their thinking. As their mental processes develop they will be able to understand that they can do things for others and others can do things for them.

Another quote from *Understanding Today's Preschoolers* helps us understand the moral development of three- and four-year-olds:

> *I judge the goodness or badness of an action by the damage done. I think it is worse to break four glasses while helping my mother set the table than to break one glass while reaching for a forbidden cookie.*
>
> *I judge the badness of an action by the severity of the punishment. If you only say, 'Now, dear, stop doing that' when I am demolishing the flower arrangement on a neighbour's table, then that is not quite as bad as my taking a flower from a vase at home for which you slap my hand.*
>
> *To me, what you stop, condemn, or punish, is wrong and what you approve, accept, or reward is right.*
>
> *This is the way my conscience develops. You stop my annoying and hurtful behaviour, and an inner voice warns me when I disobey the rules you have taught. When you laugh at what I do or give acceptance to what I do, I feel okay about continuing those behaviours. My conscience says: 'Go ahead. This is not against the rules.'* [2]

Children's willingness to accept what adults tell them is significant in terms of their spiritual development. They will believe what they are told about God. This is wonderfully positive because they can understand so many foundational truths now – God made the world, God made people, Jesus loves me, the Bible tells us how God wants us to live, and so on. But they will also believe and remember negative things they hear about God. If they hear God's name used as an expletive, or if they are threatened with 'God will get you for that', they are not helped in their understanding of God's true character.

Children may not remember many facts and details of the Bible stories they hear, but they detect atmosphere and develop attitudes which will be hard to change later. We

[2] Waldrop, C. Sybil, *Understanding Today's Preschoolers*, p. 40.

must use concrete, specific words that they can understand. If we use abstract or figurative language they will distort the meaning because the mental pictures they have for the words we are using are literal, not symbolic. If we talk about Jesus as the bread of life or the light of the world they will think literally of a loaf of bread and a lamp. They cannot understand these images yet.

Double standards

As we think through the implications of a child's moral and spiritual development there are two points I would like to make.

Firstly; we need to think carefully about how we sometimes have one standard for a child and another for ourselves. We do not allow a child to take toys from someone else, and we explain about taking turns and being kind. Yet when it is time to leave we may snatch a toy away from a child saying, 'Put that away now' without any explanation or warning. You can imagine how this appears to them. You understand that these are two different situations, but they do not. To them it appears that they are not allowed to take things from people but you are. With their limited capacity for reason and logic they cannot work this out by themselves. Even after a simple explanation they may not understand completely, but they will know, at least, that you have tried to help them understand. The very nature of the fact that adults are responsible for children means that there will be times when they have to abide by what we say, even when they don't understand. If we do our best to be consistent and provide explanations when we can, it enables them to trust us more easily in the other times.

Secondly; as you read this section on child development perhaps you learned more about how young children act, and why. This will affect the way you respond to them and interact with them. You may, however, have read some of the examples of things you might say to children and be thinking, 'This is all very well, but it sounds a bit too unreal, too nicey-nice. You don't know the children I have to deal with'. That is true. I don't know those children. But I do know my own children and the children I teach. So I know that sometimes, at the end of a busy day, or when I am tired, or when the children are particularly exasperating, I don't always respond in the best way with a smile on my face. I know that sometimes, in the heat of the moment, all my good intentions fly out the window. Many is the time that I have come away from an incident on a Sunday morning, or with my own children, and I know that I have not handled it well or responded in a right and godly way. All of this is easier to write on paper than to put into practice.

But I believe it is important to learn as much as we can about children, and have some guidelines for the most helpful ways to deal with them. At least then we have something to work towards, a general direction in which to head. Of course we will fail at times. But I would rather try and fail than have no standard at all. It may hurt to get it wrong sometimes, but without a standard you don't have the joy or satisfaction of ever knowing you got it right or succeeded.

I am thankful that I am loved by a God who knows that I won't always get it right. He knows my weaknesses and my failings. He does not stand over me with a stick, to beat me every time I am less than the best. Rather, he stands over me in love, ready to forgive, and give me his power to go on.

He has given me clear guidelines for what is right and wrong. He is patient with me and encourages me as I move on to the ultimate goal of becoming more like Jesus. And so I endeavour to do the same for the children in my care, whether they are my own, or my responsibility through teaching or child care. Knowing from the outset that I will not be perfect and that I will make mistakes actually gives me greater freedom. I am willing to try because I am not afraid of failing. With God I know there is always forgiveness and a new start.

So, be careful, and be encouraged. Be careful about consistent standards and appropriate explanations. Be encouraged that you do not have to be perfect – only willing to learn.

The first five years of a child's life are very busy indeed! They come into the world equipped with only their functioning human body and their unique genetic make-up, a combination of traits from their mother and father. As parents, teachers and care-givers we have the opportunity to influence them in terms of environment, relationships, intellectual stimulation, experiences and spiritual life. This is both an exciting and awesome responsibility. How we need God's help to adequately take up the challenge!

Chapter 7
Building the set

In any theatrical production, whether it be in the West End or the local amateur dramatic society, building the set requires careful thought and planning. Some plays have very elaborate sets, with changing colours and moving parts. Others have simple, almost understated sets, that hardly change at all during the performance. In either case, you can be sure that someone spent a lot of time thinking about how the set could enhance the performance and help to create a certain mood or atmosphere.

In the same way, we need to think carefully about the mood or atmosphere as well as the setting in which under fives can best learn. In many churches, because of limited premises or finances, we may have very little control over the physical setting in which we teach. We will look, however, at some ideas and ideals that will help us make the most of what we have.

But whatever the room is like, we do have control over the emotional and spiritual atmosphere into which the children come. In order to help us understand the kind of tone we want to set, let's look at some of the needs of all young children.

Love

Most psychologists would agree that love is a child's first need. Indeed, studies have shown that babies who have all their physical needs met but do not receive affection or love, fail to thrive, and may not even survive infancy. Even a newborn baby knows whether he is loved or rejected. Love must be constant and unchanging. It is continual, not dependent on the child behaving in a certain way. Love is not a reward for good conduct, nor should it be withheld as a punishment. To a baby, love is being fed, being kept warm, clean and dry, being cuddled when fretful, and being allowed to sleep when tired. As children grow, love is taking time to play with them, to listen to them, to answer their many questions. It is providing them with suitable activities for their stage of development. Love is giving them guidelines, but also allowing them some reasonable choices. Love is one of the greatest gifts adults can give to children. Being loved provides the foundation for them to respect themselves, to learn to love others, and to understand and accept God's love.

Each of the seven areas we are looking at now find their place in Abraham Maslow's hierarchy of needs. At the bottom of the pyramid are the physical needs. These needs, along with safety and security needs, must be met in order for survival.

MASLOW'S HIERARCHY OF NEEDS

Beyond that, the meeting of these other needs allows for actual growth as a person. Maslow envisaged a person who received not only physical care, but also love, security, trust, self-respect, etc., as one who is self-actualized. In a Christian context we might like to think of such a person as being able to grow to spiritual maturity, and use effectively the gifts and ministries God has given them. The foundations of such a life can be laid very strongly in the pre-school years.

Acceptance

Every child needs to know that their parents and other adults accept them for who they are. They want to be accepted all the time, even when adults disapprove of their behaviour. They want to be accepted for themselves, not for the things they do. If they feel they have to earn acceptance, it may result in undue submissiveness or in rebellious and outlandish behaviour in an attempt to attract attention. Knowing that they are always accepted by God is a very powerful thing as children come to understand that God loves them and accepts them just as they are.

Security

Children need to feel safe – physically and emotionally secure. Children will feel safe in an environment where there are some controls and limits. They need an adult to set boundaries to protect them from others and from their own lack of control. When children feel secure they are more able to co-operate with and think of others. If they do not feel safe, they must expend energy trying to meet their needs for security.

Children find security in relationships with parents and other adults. We want our children to have the very best. So often we express this by giving them *things*, when what they really need is *us*. As Christians we know that there is no real security in material things. As we model Christ-like relationships with children, we help them learn to find their security in God and the things of his kingdom.

Trust

As children learn to trust the adults who care for them, foundations are being laid that will enable them to trust in God. We have already looked at the way in which infants develop trust through the prompt and consistent meeting of their physical needs.

As children grow we can continue the building of that trust through our ongoing relationship with them. We listen to what they want to say to us, we help them find solutions to their problems, we correctly answer their questions and we do what we say we will do. We keep the secrets they tell us and we don't gleefully report their 'funny' mistakes for the entertainment of other adults. All these things help them to know they can trust us.

Self-respect

The way children see themselves depends on their experience of love, acceptance, security and trust. Children who have known all these things will develop self-confidence. Children who feel rejected and unloved will see themselves as unworthy and of little value. They may tend to act out what they sense those around them expect them to be. By the age of about three, children have a pretty good idea of what the adults in their lives expect of them. If adults expect them to be naughty, children will most likely live up to their expectations! If they are treated with respect and know that they are loved, they will learn to respect themselves and then treat others in the same way.

Loving and respecting children does not mean we overlook their wrong behaviour. But children are more likely to attempt to change those wrong behaviours in an environment where their efforts are met with positive affirmation and acceptance.

Dependence and independence

Children need a certain degree of independence. They need to know that there are some things they can do for themselves because they have reached that stage in their development. On the other hand, they need to know that there is an adult around who can help them when they are unable to do something. This is not always an easy balance to achieve!

Sometimes we have to let children start something by themselves, but then be ready to assist them when they are not able to complete the task. It is important for their development of independence that we let them try, even if we think they may fail. Children who are overprotected often become fearful and anxious about trying anything new. We need to create an atmosphere in which children know that they will be allowed to do that which they are able to do, but will be restrained from dangerous or destructive behaviour. Also, they will receive adult assistance when they need it without hearing, 'I told you you wouldn't be able to do it yourself!'

Discipline and guidance

We have said that children feel safe in an environment where there are some controls and limits. Research has borne this out. I remember reading a study concerning the behaviour of children in the playground of a school on a busy road. It was observed that the children played at the edges of the playground, often congregating near the fence bordering the road. When the fence was removed, leaving no boundary, the children stayed in the centre of the play area, not daring to venture near the edge. Researchers concluded that children feel safer when there are clear limits. They often test those limits, but they need to find that the limits are enforced. Children who operate in an environment where there is no control may appear on the surface to be full of bravado, and even defiant. In reality, they are often full of fears and very insecure.

Despite the evidence that children both want and need it, discipline has received a lot of bad press in recent years. Parents or teachers who advocate discipline are often regarded with scepticism or even scorn. This may be explained by a general lack of understanding about what discipline really is. It is often mistakenly associated with harsh punishment and tyrannical dictatorship!

True discipline implies learning. Just as the word 'disciple' indicates one who is learning to be a follower, so discipline implies a process of learning. As an adult disciplines a child, the child learns (sometimes after many attempts!) to be responsible for his own behaviour. The ultimate goal is that the discipline will come from within – it will result from self-control rather than external forces. Children are not born with self-discipline or the ability to control their own actions. It is the responsibility of their parents and other significant adults in their lives (for example, teachers) to set limits and controls that are maintained with love, consistency, clarity and patience. In this kind of relationship a child can learn self-control.

In addition to discipline a child needs guidance – in knowing how to be safe, in learning to relate to other people, and in developing various skills. In guidance and in discipline we may find it helpful to remember that the kind of help a child needs is related to that child's temperament and current stage of development. It is important to realize that what works with one child may not work with another. Whatever approach we may use it is necessary to be consistent and clear in our expectations in order to avoid confusing the child.

We must also be realistic – expecting too much too soon, or setting guidelines that are beyond a child's capability sets them up for failure and discourages them. We need to help children experience success more often than failure.

When children come into a room where the teachers understand their basic needs and are aware of their level of development, they are more able to learn what the teachers want to teach them. They are creating an atmosphere that is conducive to learning. They have already built the most important part of the set.

But what about the room itself? What should it be like? What equipment should we have? How big should it be? The room isn't everything ('That's a relief!', I can hear you say) but it does help, and we want to make it the best that we possibly can. How do we do it?

What's in a room?

I have taught under fives in a variety of settings. My first experiences were in America, where churches are purpose-built, rooms are often large, light and airy and, chances are, the room is not used for any other age group. I have also used cold church halls that were twice the size they needed to be, and small, crowded rooms that were half the size they needed to be! I have used a village playgroup room where some of the equipment was 'off limits' to us and school classrooms where the floors have been trampled by children's dirty shoes for days. I have even used gardens and parks as my main classroom! Some of the

81

venues I have used have had everything I needed, others have had next to nothing.

A room that is perfectly equipped, meeting every specification is not a guarantee for good teaching. If the teachers are not prepared and are not genuine in their desire to teach, all the finest supplies in the world won't make any difference. On the other hand, a room that is bare, with almost no appropriate toys or supplies can be turned into a place of much joyful learning by a teacher who understands the children and wants to show them something of God.

I had this confirmed to me recently when my husband and I were in Kenya. We had the opportunity of ministering at a conference for missionaries. With no advance notice, I found myself with about half a dozen three- and four-year-olds each morning for just over an hour. There was a large room and a basket of toys that had been provided for use with babies and toddlers in an earlier session. The only art supplies were paper, crayons and a glue stick. What an excellent opportunity to test all my theories!

I chose the theme, 'God made . . .', and each day we talked about something different that God made. We had a wonderful time! Thanks to the African weather we were able to spend some time learning outside each day. We borrowed a big cooking pot from the kitchen one morning and had lots of fun finding out what kinds of things float and what sinks to the bottom. Another day we borrowed a large tray and my husband's shaving foam and had a great time finger painting!

In four sessions we had time to develop a nice relationship, and I looked forward to each day as much as they did. It was our special time, and they knew it. Although I am sure that none of them will remember that week by the time they are fifteen I am also sure that it was part of the ongoing process of foundation building in their lives. I think it was a great encouragement to their parents, as well.

If it is the teacher who makes the difference, is it worth

making a fuss about the physical premises? Well, a man can survive on bread and water. Does that mean he shouldn't ask for fruit and vegetables? We should be encouraged that ultimately it is we as parents and teachers that enable learning to take place. But we should also do what we can to make the room work for us.

In many churches the work among children is severely limited by the premises. There may only be a main meeting area, with little or no extra space. We have already mentioned the possibility of utilising nearby homes, schools or halls for classroom space. If none of this is viable on a Sunday, perhaps the church will need to adopt a more family style approach to Sunday worship and attempt to provide age-related teaching at some point during the week. Obviously, this is a very difficult situation which requires much creative thinking. If no formal structures can be developed, perhaps parents with children of similar ages could join together to provide a group learning experience in the home during the week.

Every church is in a unique situation. Therefore, speaking in general terms can sometimes be unhelpful. Churches in particularly awkward circumstances can feel frustrated at their seeming inability to implement anything of what they want to do. Those who find themselves in that kind of situation may find it best to seek advice from an individual who can assess their setting in detail and provide suggestions specific to them.

For the purposes of this book we must work on the assumption that some kind of room or meeting place is available. What is the ideal? The size of a room should be related to the number and ages of the children using it. For instance: where children from birth to five are together, one large room could accommodate up to ten children. If there are more than ten children it might be better to divide them into two groups, maybe birth to two, and three to five. They could either use two smaller rooms, or divide a large one between them. It may be possible to purchase some dividing screens, or have someone in the church make some tall, folding room dividers.

The older the children, the larger the group can be. A fairly big room could be suitable for fifteen three- to five-year-olds. (By fairly big I mean at least 15 ft × 15 ft.) A group that size of toddlers, would be difficult to manage, even in a large space. More teaching can take place if they are divided into two groups of seven or eight children.

Putting too many children into a room is likely to lead to problems. Under fives are just learning to get along with others. Being in a room with a large number of children means being close to a lot of other people who want the same things they want. Bumps and collisions are bound to happen.

Many day nurseries have large numbers of children together in one room without too many difficulties. When play is the main objective, that is fine. But for adults to have the opportunity for more meaningful interaction with individual children, and for teaching to take place, smaller groups work better with younger children.

If it is not possible to divide large groups, it is helpful to divide the room into different and distinct interest areas, with a teacher in each area. The children may move from area to area, but the toys or equipment stay in their designated space. This means that each teacher will only be dealing with a limited number of children at any one time. In the section on 'How to teach' we will develop the idea of using various interest areas for teaching.

People have differing ideas about what a classroom for under fives should look like. Many have visions of teddy bears and clowns painted on the walls, and all the latest in educational toys available around the room. What we actually encounter in most churches is a far cry from that. When a room is going to be used by two-year-olds on Sunday, the Boys Brigade on Tuesday, and the young peoples' group on Friday, teddy bears and clowns may not go down too well! In fact, even if the room is only used by young children, plain walls are probably best. The attraction is supposed to be the teaching activities provided, not the walls. Because a young child has difficulty in distinguishing fact from fantasy it is best to stick with reality at church anyway. So don't worry about the walls – clean, light colours are better than fancy murals.

If tables and chairs are a problem, forget them. Children under two don't need them anyway, and even with threes and fours most activities can be done just as well on the floor. It is better (and safer!) to use the floor than to use adult size tables and chairs. Push all adult furniture to the edges of the room to make as much floor space as possible. If the floor is rough or cold, carpet scraps may be necessary. Many carpet shops will give you reasonably sized remnants or ends of roll for a small price, or even free, if they know what you want them for. Activities like artwork that require hard surfaces can be done on large trays.

Now, what about equipment? How many times have you seen a church crèche that is the dumping ground for everyone's old, unused or broken toys? The floor is often a clutter of mismatched toys, none of which contain all the bits. They are often stored in boxes which appear just to be tipped out in the middle of the floor at the beginning of each session. No wonder the children find it hard to settle and play. A junky pile of toys is not very inviting, and they find it very frustrating when the toy they want to play with has some pieces missing. It is far better to have a few, well-chosen toys, carefully placed, than a room full of bits and pieces.

It is important that the toys be appropriate for the age of the child. Hence, small pieces are not safe for babies who are still putting everything into their mouths. That is why dividing a room of mixed age groups is helpful. One part of the room can contain toys suitable for babies and toddlers, and the other part can house the toys for older pre-schoolers.

For babies and very young toddlers, bright simple toys are best. Rattles, balls and large wooden bricks can be used in a variety of ways. As toddlers progress, nesting and stacking toys are excellent. Simple puzzles with large pieces prove popular. Toys that can be pulled by a string are useful for those children who are walking.

Two-year-olds and up enjoy items that enable them to pretend about the home. These would include a simple doll, a doll bed, plastic dishes, a pretend cooker and so on. These items do not mean spending a lot of money. Many of them can be made or improvised and some can be bought quite inexpensively from markets and 'junk' shops.

Contrary to popular belief, slides, climbing frames and bikes are not a particularly good idea. They often encourage loud rough play, and can lead to accidents. There are other ways of channelling extra energy more fruitfully.

Simple toys that encourage creativity are the best. You can't beat a good set of wooden bricks for endless use. For older children, toys that fit together like Duplo and stickle bricks are useful. It is best to avoid toys that specifically direct a child's play or that involve characters that are not real. For instance: puzzles should feature realistic pictures rather than Thomas the Tank Engine or teddy bears dancing. There is nothing wrong with these things, but in church it is important to deal with what is real. If a child is hearing stories or working puzzles about Postman Pat or Rupert Bear one minute, and the next he is hearing a Bible story, he will not know which is true and which is not. It is important for him to know that everything his teacher tells him about is true.

Likewise, toys such as Thunderbirds or My Little Pony tell a child what to play rather than letting him use his imagination and develop his creativity. While these toys may have their place in the home, they may not be the most effective for teaching at church.

Bricks, home play items and stacking toys are not too difficult to find, but suitable books and puzzles can be more of a problem. Whenever I go anywhere that has these things, I keep my eyes open — especially in sales!

Much more detail will be given about toys when we look at the different teaching areas. Suggestions will be given for making some things at almost no cost. If you are needing to acquire some equipment for your under fives, it might be most helpful to make specific requests about what you need, rather than just asking people to donate old toys. You could ask for a set of wooden bricks, or some Duplo. You might even suggest that someone who wants to contribute to this vital area of ministry may like to give some money for the purchase of new equipment! Some churches make allowance in their budgets for work among different age groups, and the church treasurer may be able to help you.

Remember, it is the teacher who makes a room. Do your best to make it clean and light. Provide simple toys in an uncluttered fashion. Have one or two different and interesting activities each week. Make the most of what you have, then forget about it and get on with teaching. It is you the children will respond to.

Building the set for learning with under fives is absolutely crucial to the action of the play that is to take place. As far as we are able, we must make the most of the physical facilities we have. More importantly, though, we must set the right atmosphere. This can be done by understanding the needs of young children, and knowing where they are in terms of their development.

We are helped to provide the right variety of activities as we understand how under fives learn. In the next section we will look at seven key ways in which learning happens.

Chapter 8

How do under fives learn?

Under fives are always learning! Because of the vast amount they must accomplish in the first five years of life, there is no time to waste! For older children and adults, learning is often narrowly defined in terms of books, writing and tests that measure what they have taken in. This is not at all the case for a young child. All of life is the classroom, and all their experiences are the teacher. The exams are not written. Learning is measured by their development – physically, mentally, emotionally and spiritually. They learn in a number of ways.

Relationships

Through relationships with adults and others children acquire facts and information, but they also learn feelings and attitudes. To a young child actions and attitudes speak far louder than words. Children may hear the words 'share' and 'be nice', but if they do not see these words being acted out towards them and others, they will learn their own ways of dealing with people from the attitudes they have seen demonstrated rather than the words they have heard spoken.

In the same way, a child who hears the words 'I love you' accompanied by gentle affection, a warm smile and a kind voice, learns about appropriate ways to express love.

Children learn a lot about themselves through relationships. They sense whether they are loved, valued and respected. A significant part of their self-image is determined by relationships rather than words. A teacher who is able to say all the right words, but not able to develop warm and caring relationships with children is not helpful. A teacher who conveys interest through facial expression, time spent with children and attention to their needs is far more effective. Sometimes the most important learning takes place when no one is aware of it and without a word being spoken.

Children also learn attitudes through relationships. A young child does not naturally fear or dislike a child from a different racial or ethnic group. That attitude is learned from others. Children will not consistently manipulate others to meet their own needs unless someone has demonstrated to them that using others is an effective means of getting what they want.

Children learn far more than we realize through relationships. Feelings and attitudes about themselves and others are more often 'caught' than 'taught'.

Physical senses

All that we learn is taken in through one of our five senses. For a newborn baby, touch may be the most significant of the senses. As hearing develops they learn to distinguish one voice from another, and pleasant sounds from unpleasant. As vision becomes clearer they recognize familiar faces and objects. Even taste and smell are important early on. They know the smell of their mother, and of milk or formula. They taste the milk, and as solid food is introduced they respond to new and exciting tastes.

Children learn much about the world around them through their senses. They learn about hard and soft, hot and cold, safe and unsafe through touching. They learn about objects by seeing them, touching them, and even tasting them. A child can learn much by smelling different foods or flowers. As children hear different sounds, they learn to recognize them and distinguish where they are coming from. Most children enjoy listening to music. We can help children learn by stimulating and developing their senses.

Imitating

Children imitate what they see and hear others doing. They watch others use knives, forks and spoons and they learn how to feed themselves. They hear others speaking and they learn to talk. If they see others hitting and acting violently, they will imitate that as well. If they hear shouting, harshness and rude language they will copy it. Children imitate as a means of learning. They also imitate as a means of play. Children may pretend to talk on the telephone, wash dishes, drive a car or play a sport. Which parent has not laughed one minute and cringed the next as they see or hear their children imitating them?

Children learn a lot by imitating. Unfortunately, in their first few years they do not have the ability to distinguish between those things it is good to imitate and those things they should not copy. As parents and teachers we need to be careful to give them something good and positive to imitate.

Curiosity

Children are born curious! Even very young babies turn their heads to see and hear what is going on around them. As they grow, they examine everything in sight by touching, tasting, shaking, hitting or even throwing it!

As they learn to talk they may ask many questions. Why does it make that noise? What is this for? Sometimes it is difficult to be patient in answering so many questions. Other times we may not know the answer to the questions. Why is it raining when I want to play in the garden? Which is nearer — heaven or space? Most adults don't like to admit they don't know the answer, but a child is helped more by our honesty than a made-up, incorrect answer. Providing toys and activities that arouse and stimulate their God-given curiosity helps children learn.

Answering children's questions can often prove difficult and time consuming. It is important, though, because it helps them to know we are interested in them, and encourages them to continue to be motivated by curiosity. We should always be truthful (even when that means saying, 'I don't know the answer to that question'), give accurate answers, and keep the explanations at a level the child can understand.

We also need to make sure we know just what it is the child is asking so that we answer what they want to know.

Once a young child came and asked his father, 'Dad, where did I come from?' His father had been dreading this inevitable day, so he drew a deep breath and then gave his son a detailed explanation about the facts of life. Afterwards he asked, 'Son, what made you ask that question?' The boy shrugged and replied, 'Well, the new girl next door says she comes from Yorkshire and I just wondered where I came from?'

Curiosity is healthy and it is the beginning of discovery. Children learn as we encourage their natural urge to explore and ask questions.

Repetition

Learning requires memory and memory needs developing. That is why repetition plays such an important role in learning for the under fives. Read it again! Sing it again! Do it again! Often we tire of it — but they don't! As they hear a song over and over again, they learn the words. As they work a puzzle many times, they learn how the pieces fit together.

I have recently started teaching one- to two-year-olds on Sunday mornings, and each week I sing different songs that develop the teaching theme for that day. But each week I have also done the same simple finger play two or three times. The first week they just watched me in amazement. Now, after four or five weeks, the older ones can do it themselves. They have learned through repetition. Even with three- to five-year-olds I find that if we have time at the end of Group Time and I ask them what they want to sing, they always choose the same songs.

Children acquire new skills through repetition. A toddler cannot drink from a cup without spilling the first time he tries. He must do it over and over again to get it right. He needs to be encouraged in his attempts to master new tasks.

Doing

Children learn best through firsthand experiences. They learn by doing. We can talk to a child about Spring. We can look at pictures and books. But a very young child learns the most about Spring as we point out the daffodils pushing their way up through the soil, as we notice buds on trees and bushes, and as we listen for the birds singing in the morning.

Children also enjoy doing things for themselves. We need to plan activities that they can do. If an art activity is so difficult that we have to do the work for them, then they will not learn. They have a sense of satisfaction in what they can accomplish themselves. If we provide an activity that has to be glued, folded or coloured in a certain way in order to turn out 'right', children may feel that they cannot produce something that is acceptable unless it is just like the one the teacher made.

With under fives, the fun and the learning in most activities is in the doing, not in the finished product. So if a three-year-old is painting, it does not matter what it looks like. The important thing is that they did it themselves, and that someone encouraged their efforts.

When a young child is gluing, they may need help spreading the glue, but they can stick the picture on the paper themselves. It doesn't matter to them if it is upside down or crooked, unless they have heard an adult tell them they must put it on in a certain way.

Providing 'doing' activities for under fives is important. This can prove very time-consuming in the home for parents and other carers, but it is a vital part of their learning. At church, teachers can provide activities that enable children to learn through doing, and to derive satisfaction from their growing independence.

Play

Play is work to children. It is their natural way of learning. When they play they can practise new skills, experiment with many different materials, discover, pretend, and create. As they play with others they learn social skills, how to relate to others, how to take turns and share, and how to solve problems. Because play is their natural activity it provides countless opportunities for conveying spiritual truth, and teaching biblical principles.

If a casual observer were to walk into any class of under fives in our church they might say, 'They are only playing'. They are playing, but as they play we are teaching them the things of God. We may tell them the Bible says 'Be kind'. As two children take turns with the same toy they are learning how to relate this Bible truth to life. We may tell children how to behave. Play gives them the opportunity to practise what we have said.

Understanding that under fives learn through relationships, the physical senses, imitating, curiosity, repetition, doing, and play helps us to provide activities that maximize the time we have with them at church. Developing a relationship with each child we teach, stimulating the physical senses, and being an example worth imitating all help children learn the right things. Encouraging their curiosity, providing many of the same activities, songs and stories again and again, and letting them do what they can for themselves helps us to teach effectively. Guiding 'hands-on', here-and-now experiences through play enables us to show them how to apply the truths of God's word to their lives.

Children can learn in many ways. Wise teachers try to make the best use of all of them.

Chapter 9

What can under fives learn about God?

What to teach

When teaching the under fives is mentioned, the first question many people ask is, 'What do you teach them?' When the subject of 'Sunday School' comes up, most people have a mental picture of a group experience. They think of a circle of children being told a Bible story, singing songs or quoting Bible verses together. This picture does not work with babies or two-year-olds – no wonder they ask the question!

The key to the answer lies in defining teaching and learning. A young child can reel off a long list of facts and statements that he has memorized, to the amazement of the adults around him. Because his language ability exceeds his thinking ability we may be fooled into believing that he knows what he is talking about. He may actually have no understanding whatsoever. If that is the case, what has he learned? Learning is far more than just the memorizing of facts. It implies understanding those facts, developing skills and using ideas. Learning will affect more than just the mind. It may involve changes in feelings, attitudes and concepts.

In the same way, good teaching is more than just the passing on of information. It is the imparting of knowledge and the ability to use that knowledge. I remember a certain lecturer at university whose style was less than inspiring. He turned up for lectures and basically read various portions of the textbook to us. He did not tell us anything we couldn't read for ourselves. I do not think it would be too harsh to say that he did not teach us anything. And I don't think we learned much either! I also remember another lecturer who made the textbook come alive for us. In fact, I read many pages of pathophysiology without being any the wiser for it. Then I attended his lecture and he explained what I had read so that I was able to understand quite clearly. Not only that, he always gave us practical examples of how we could use our knowledge in different situations we would encounter on the hospital wards. He was a real teacher, and from him we learned a great deal.

What do we teach under fives at church? The obvious, simple answer is the Bible. But teaching the Bible involves far more than just telling and re-telling stories until children remember them. It is more than games designed to memorize lots of verses. Effective teaching of the Bible with under fives means using its stories and verses in ways they can understand and relate to their own world. It means teaching them to say, 'Be kind to one another', and then providing an activity which gives them the chance to be kind. We want to teach them not only to know what the Bible says, but to be able to do it as well.

Helping children to remember Bible stories and say Bible verses is important. But it is more important to help them understand and apply its basic truths. It is perfectly possible to teach a three-year-old to recite the Beatitudes (Matthew 5) or the fruits of the Spirit (Galatians 5). They can learn to say the words. But because of their limited mental processes and their inability to understand figurative or picture language, they will not understand what they are saying. We may think they have learned an important passage of Scripture. What they might actually have learned is that the Bible is for quoting, not for understanding. They may have learned that saying the right words earns adult approval, or a star on their chart. Without meaning to, we may be laying the foundation for them to go through life quoting the Bible and reading its stories without ever learning to do what it says.

If we want our children to grow up not only knowing about the Bible, but also understanding it and applying it to their lives, how do we go about it? The Bible is a difficult enough book for adults. How can we possibly teach it to young children, even babies, who can only think literally, don't understand symbolism and are not yet able to use reason and logic? Can we make the Bible meaningful for them? The task seems overwhelming, if not impossible.

Be encouraged. It is possible, and an exciting challenge. Let's look at eight different foundational areas that we can use to teach basic biblical truths to even the youngest of children. In each area we will look at the basic concepts that under fives can learn and what our teaching aims and objectives might be.

God

Babies and toddlers can learn that:
- *God is a name* We provide opportunities for each child to hear God's name in a warm and positive way.
- *God is a person* Each child hears about the ways that God is good to them; they hear the words, 'God loves you'; they hear their teachers say, 'Thank you, God . . .'

Two- and three-year-olds can also understand that:
- *God made people* We help each child become aware that God made them and others.
- *God loves people* Each child hears that God loves them; they become more aware of ways that God shows his love for people.
- *God wants people to love him* Each child hears of ways that people show their love for God.
- *People talk to God* We help each child express thanks to God; we provide opportunities for each child to hear their teachers talk to God, and for them to talk to God.
- *God wants people to love and help each other* Each child hears about ways that people can help each other; we provide opportunities for them to help others.
- *God made the world* Each child becomes aware that God made plants, animals, earth, sky, etc.; we provide opportunities for them to explore things God made; we provide opportunities for them to help care for plants and animals.

Four- and five-year-olds can learn that:
- *God cares for people* Each child grows in their understanding that God provides and cares for people.
- *God can do things that people cannot do* Each child has an increased awareness that God can do things people cannot do.
- *God wants people to worship him and thank him* We help each child understand that God wants people to worship him (read the Bible, pray, sing, tell him we love him); we provide opportunities for them to worship and thank God, because God is good.
- *God wants people to talk to him* Each child becomes aware that they can talk to God any time and any place and that God hears our prayers any time.
- *God wants people everywhere to learn about him* Each child is more aware that God wants people to learn about him.

Natural world

Babies and toddlers learn that:
- *God made things that we can see, touch, taste, smell and hear* We provide opportunities for children to explore and discover things that God made.
- *God made the animals* Each child sees pictures of animals and hears that God made the animals.

Two- and three-year-olds can also understand that:
- *God made the world and he provides food for people and animals* Each child hears about the plants and animals God made; we help them associate God's name with nature.

Four- and five-year-olds learn that:
- *God made sun, moon, stars, snow, rain, wind, day and night* Each child grows in their understanding that God showed his love by making the natural world.
- *God wants people, animals and plants to grow* We provide opportunities for each child to see how plants, animals and people grow.

- *God wants people to care for the things he made* Each child becomes more aware that the things God made need care, and that they can help care for them.

Jesus

Babies and toddlers can begin to understand that:

- *Jesus is a name* We provide opportunities for each child to hear the name of Jesus used warmly and positively.
- *Jesus is a person* Each child sees pictures and hears stories about Jesus as a baby, child and man; they hear the words, 'Jesus loves you'; they have a growing awareness that Jesus helped others and that Jesus is a special person.

Two- and three-year-olds can add to that understanding by learning:

- *Jesus was born, he grew, he had a family who cared for him* We help each child associate the birth of Jesus with Christmas; we help them realize that Jesus grew up and that he was part of a family.
- *Jesus loves people and wants people to love him* Each child will hear that Jesus loves them and other people, and will hear Bible stories about the way Jesus showed his love for people; they will hear about people in the Bible who loved Jesus, and about people today who love Jesus.
- *Jesus wants people to love and help each other* We provide opportunities for each child to hear about ways people help each other; we provide activities that enable them to help others.

Four- and five-year-olds can learn that:

- *Jesus is God's Son* Each child will develop more awareness that Jesus is God's Son and that God showed his love by sending Jesus.
- *Jesus helped people because he loved them* We help each child begin to understand that not only did Jesus help people in the Bible who needed his help, but Jesus loves and helps them, too.
- *Jesus can do things that people cannot do*

Self

Babies and toddlers can understand that:

● *I am a person*   We provide opportunities for each child to hear that God made him, God planned for him to grow, God gave him different parts of his body so that he can do different things; he begins to sense that he is special because God made him; we allow him to begin to make simple choices when appropriate (like which book to look at or which toy to play with).

Two- and three-year-olds can also learn that:

● *I am growing and I can do many things*   Each child becomes more aware that God planned for and helps him to grow; he associates his ability to do things with God.

● *I am a special person*   Each child discovers that he is special to other people and that he is accepted and loved by others; he becomes more aware that God loves him and that God made each person special and different.

Four- and five-year-olds go on to understand that:

● *I am important to God, others and myself*   We help each child realize that not only is he important to God and others, but to have a sense of self-worth also.

● *I can make choices*   We provide opportunities for each child to make choices when appropriate, and help him express his feelings, attitudes and actions positively through those choices.

● *I can take turns and share*   Each child has specific opportunities to share and take turns with others.

Family

Babies and toddlers can learn that:

● *I have a family*   Each child becomes aware that God made families; they hear about ways that Christian family members show their love; they associate warm feelings with their family. (It needs to be said here that the whole subject of family life raises many questions and problems in these days of fractured families. We want to teach God's plan and intention for families accurately, yet sensitively. (See 'Happy Families?' p. 28.)

Two- and three-year-olds learn that:
- *God planned for family members to love and help each other* We help each child understand that being part of a family is God's plan for people.
- *Other people are in my family* We help each child to feel that they are a significant person in their family.
- *I can help my family* Each child becomes aware of ways they can help their family.

Four- and five-year-olds can move on to understand that:
- *God wants people to live, work and play together in families* We help each child to understand this in the context of their own family situation.
- *Each person in a family has their own possessions and jobs to do* Each child begins to understand that others in their family have things that belong to them, and that different family members have different responsibilities.
- *The Bible has stories about families* We provide opportunities for each child to hear Bible stories about families that love and help one another.

Church

Babies and toddlers learn that:
- *People love me and take care of me at church* We help each child feel loved, cared for and secure at church; we help each child enjoy being at church.
- *People sing and talk about God and Jesus at church* We provide opportunities for each child to hear teachers sing and talk about God and Jesus.
- *There are lots of things for me to do at church* We provide a variety of learning activities for each child.

Two- and three-year-olds can learn that:
- *I have friends at church* We help each child be aware of friends at church who love them; each child will feel

happy and secure with their friends at church; each child will feel that they are a significant person at church.

- *People at church help others* We provide opportunities for each child to hear Bible stories about people who helped at church and to hear of ways that people help at church today; we give each child opportunities to help at church.

Four- and five-year-olds also understand that:
- *At church we sing songs, use the Bible and learn about God and Jesus* Each child becomes aware of the importance of the things we do at church.
- *Going to church is important* We help each child understand that being part of a church is what God wants for people.
- *People at church have different jobs to do* The child becomes aware that although people at church have different kinds of jobs to do, we all work together to help other people learn about God and Jesus.
- *People go to different church buildings* We help each child learn that there are other churches besides theirs.

The Bible

Babies and toddlers can begin to understand that:
- *The Bible is a special book* Each child has opportunities to see and touch the Bible.
- *The Bible tells about Jesus* We provide opportunities for each child to hear stories about Jesus when the Bible is used.

Two- and three-year-olds can learn that:
- *The Bible has stories and verses about God, Jesus and people* We help each child have an increasing desire to hear stories from the Bible.

Four- and five-year-olds can also understand that:
- *The Bible is an important book* Each child sees teachers and other adults at church handle and use the Bible frequently.

Sharing Jesus with under fives

- *The Bible helps us to know how God wants us to live* We help each child to hear stories and verses from the Bible that tell how to treat other people; we help each child become aware that Bible truths relate to their everyday life.

Others
Babies and toddlers can begin to understand that:
- *People love me and take care of my needs* We help each child become aware that other people take care of them.
- *I am aware of other people* Each child becomes more aware of other people around them and enjoys being with other people.

Two- and three-year-olds learn that:
- *Other people love and help me* We talk to each child about the ways other people care for them.
- *I can love and help others* We help each child to learn ways that they can be kind and loving to others.

Four- and five-year-olds move on to learn that:
- *I can be considerate of other people* We help each child become aware that each person has feelings.
- *Some things belong to me and some things belong to others* We help each child to grow in their understanding that not everything belongs to them.
- *God (Jesus) wants people to love and help each other* Each child has opportunities to learn ways that they can help others.
- *People are alike in some ways and different in some ways* We help each child understand that although we are alike in many ways, God has made each one of us different.
- *God planned for us to have friends* Each child grows in their understanding of what it means to be a friend.

Perhaps this list is much longer than you expected it to be! You may have doubts about whether any child under five can learn all of this. It might even seem more sensible to stop reading now, rather than try to wade any further into this impossible task!

Yes, the list is long and fairly comprehensive. So is the Bible – there is a lot to teach! Of course, each child will grasp these foundational areas at their own pace and according to their own capabilities. And even the brightest of children would not be able to recount each of these truths as we have written them here. Remember, learning is not measured by what children can say, but by what they understand and can put to use. It is very nice to *hear* children say, 'God wants us to love and help each other', but it is far better to *see* them help another child with a difficult puzzle or assist the teacher in putting the bricks away at the end of the session!

It never ceases to amaze me just how much young children can and do learn. The task of building these foundational truths into their lives *is* daunting, but it is also very rewarding to see them growing up knowing the love of God in their lives.

We have looked at *what* we can teach the under fives in terms of spiritual truth. Now let us go on to look at *how* we go about teaching these things. We will look at different activities we might use and the kinds of things we might say in order to turn these activities into teaching opportunities.

Chapter 10
Teaching through activities

At last, we come to the 'how to' section. All that we have said thus far is crucial as a foundation for understanding this practical material. If we had started here, without first looking at why we teach, how children learn and develop, and what things we can teach them, these activities would have given you ideas, but not actually helped you to teach. Now that we have increased our understanding (and, hopefully, our vision!) we are ready to put it into practice.

In working with under fives, the most effective way to communicate all that we have talked about in the previous chapters is through the use of various activities. All of them are different forms of play, but each has a purpose and aim. This transforms them from simply play into teaching/learning activities.

We will look at several different activities and how they can be used to teach biblical truth. Not all of these activity areas can, or should, be used every week. Some of them, however, do need to be offered each time in order to give some sense of continuity and security. Children like to know that certain things will be there every time they come to church, but they also need at least one or two different activities each week to stimulate their interest.

The number of activities you provide is largely dependent on the number of teachers you have. Some activity areas require little adult supervision. Others need an adult present at all times. If you are the only teacher in the room, rather than only providing one activity at a time and then moving on to the next one, it is probably better to have a few low-supervision activities available with one teacher-led activity. When all the children who want to have participated in that activity it can be put away and something else provided.

In a room where there are two teachers, it may still be

as well to have only one teacher-led activity. This leaves the second teacher free to supervise the other activities in a general way, and specifically interact with children, one or two at a time, as they play.

The idea behind providing a variety of activities at the same time is to enable the children to make choices about what they do. Learning to make choices and live with the consequences of those choices is part of their development. Allowing them to make non-life-threatening choices in this environment is a foundation for making more important choices later.

No two children are alike, and what one child chooses to do will be different from what the next child chooses. If children are allowed to select an activity that interests them, they will find it a much more enjoyable and productive learning experience. Giving young children the opportunity to be involved in various activities at the same time recognizes not only their different interests, but also their maturity level.

Once children reach school age they begin to learn by all being involved in the same activity at the same time. Before school age, however, asking them to do this seems unnecessary and not particularly helpful in creating a happy learning environment. Any teacher who has tried to organize a group of three- or four-year-olds to all do the same thing at the same time knows that there is always at least one who wants to do something else!

Let's look, then, at what activities we might provide for under fives. In this 'how to' section there are eight major activity areas that can be used in teaching the under fives. The possible variations for each activity are numerous. Even if four or five activity areas are provided for three- and four-year-olds each Sunday, there are enough ideas to last for several months. Unlike older children, under fives do not need something new and different every week. They need some things to stay the same, to give them security. They need a few things to be different each week in order to stimulate their interest. Getting the balance right is part of learning to teach.

Babies and toddlers also benefit from these activity areas. Although they may be content simply to play with toys week by week, we can give them more positive spiritual input as they play by using these ideas.

Chapter 11
Art

The purpose of art

Art materials are anything that a child can use to make something of his own. The most important part of any art activity is the process, not the finished product. An art activity should be fun, and provide the child with the satisfaction of saying, 'I made it myself!'

What is the purpose of art activity? Is it to make a picture that illustrates the Bible story? Is it to take home something which parents will enjoy looking at? Is it to fill time in the session? Of course, it is none of these. Art is a means of allowing children to express themselves creatively and to experiment with different materials. It allows children to have a sense of accomplishment. On a physical level, it develops the dexterity of small muscles in the hands and arms. Socially, it provides opportunities for children to work alongside others, learn to wait for their turn, and share supplies.

If art is to achieve all these things, it must be used carefully and in a variety of forms. Whatever form the activity takes each week, certain guidelines can help us to make it an enjoyable and rewarding experience for the children.

Can the children work on their own?

The activity needs to be something the children can do for themselves, with only a little guidance from the teacher. If you have to do most of the work, the activity is too difficult.

Avoid having a finished product in mind

This is probably the most common mistake made in working with under fives and art. Adults come up with marvellous ideas for illustrating the Bible story, but the project is too difficult and too restricting for the child. The teacher may spend hours cutting out various shapes and pieces that are to be put together in a certain way to produce the finished product. He then has to stand over every child to make sure that each piece is glued 'the right way'. When it is finished, it may look very nice, but the child has not made the picture, the teacher has. The child has not created anything. The parents might think it is very wonderful as well, but they are praising the teacher's creativity, not their child's work. So often, we devise art projects that satisfy us, as adults, rather than the children we are teaching.

Look for ways to make each child succeed

Whatever art activity you choose for a session, make sure that each child's work is praised. For instance, if the story is about David looking after his father's sheep, avoid the temptation to provide the outline of a sheep for children to colour in – many of them do not yet have the muscular control necessary to stay within the lines. Even gluing cotton wool balls onto the outline will be too difficult for some children. If they think that you want the picture to look a certain way, they will feel they have failed if they cannot do it. Some may not even try, in order to avoid failure. Rather, provide cotton wool balls and wool scraps for children to create their own collage. As they work, you will be able to talk with them about David and the sheep. As they take turns with the glue or assist another child, you can talk about the fact that David was a helper and they are being helpers. Whatever each child's picture looks like, it will be a success. They took time over it, they enjoyed the process, and they had a sense of independence because they made it themselves. Those are the things you praise, rather than the appearance of the picture.

Avoid comparing children's work

Some children may well be able to draw recognizable shapes, paint a specific object or cut neatly with scissors. Others of the same age may not. Each child's work must be accepted without comparison to another's. There is no 'right' way to paint a picture or glue a collage. A child can be made to feel inadequate if his work is held up alongside someone else's for comment. I have heard teachers say, 'Let's see who can make the best picture today.' No doubt this comment is meant to encourage the children to do their best. Unfortunately, it actually creates the impression that some work is more acceptable than others. Children under five don't need that kind of pressure. There is enough of that as they get older and go to school. At this age, we need to help them 'succeed' as often as we can.

Provide art experiences that encourage creative expression

As adults, we gain satisfaction in terms of end results or finished product. I may feel satisfied when I look at my house, clean and tidy after a day of busyness. You may feel a sense of achievement as you hand your boss a file that represents a few weeks of concentrated research and contains some exciting new ideas. Young children are not like that. They derive pleasure and learn in the process of doing and making, not in the product which results. They may be excited as they come out of their class, waving a picture and saying, 'Look what I made!' But most of the benefit is in the actual process involved and the appreciation expressed by the adults in their lives, not in sitting afterwards and gazing at their picture. So we need to make art materials available, with some guidance about how to use them, then let the children get on with it. It is better to give them time to be creative and not worry so much about what it looks like in the end.

This is often very difficult for us as adults. We can easily be so concerned with what something looks like that we forget the point of the exercise. For most birthdays of friends and relatives, I encourage my children to make cards. Not only does it save money, but I believe it helps my children to understand about the thought behind sending cards. So often, though, I slip into trying to dictate to them what the card should look like. I want it to be pleasing to me more than I want it to be an expression of their creativity. Only the other day they were making birthday cards for my mother in America. They were looking through the supply of old birthday and Christmas cards we have received to find pictures to cut out and stick on to their paper. Samuel, who is nearly three, chose a distinctly Christmas picture. I tried to persuade him that this was not appropriate for a birthday card in May, but he was insistent. I suddenly realized that I was denying him the chance to make his own card the way he wanted it, just because I was concerned with what my mother would think of me! I am quite sure that my mother will be delighted to receive cards that represent the careful and loving work of her grandchildren. She is more interested in the fact that they know it's her birthday than in what the cards look like!

Sometimes it is not easy, but we must learn to provide experiences that are of benefit more to the children than to us.

Before using a new idea, try it yourself!

This will avoid embarrassment for you and disappointment for the children when the clever idea you've come up with doesn't actually work! Trying it out for yourself also helps you find out whether the children will be able to do it, or if it is too complicated. Lots of the art activities we do are great fun even for adults. Having a go at home means that I can enjoy the experience, too, without taking time away from the children during the session.

Never ask, 'What is it?'

Chances are that most of them haven't made a picture of anything, but as soon as you ask the question, they think, 'Oh dear! I have to think of something fast. Teacher asked me what it is, and it really wasn't anything, but she wants it to be something. What can it be?' A statement such as, 'Andrew, you have worked very hard on your picture today. Would you like to tell me about it?' allows the child to say as much or as little as he wants. Comments like;

'Jennifer, you have used the glue very carefully today. May I look at your picture?' help a child to know that you noticed her efforts with the glue and that you are interested in her work. It is better to avoid statements that attach worth to the picture, like; 'This is a good picture, James.' or 'That's a very good house, Abigail. Aren't you clever?' This may cause the child to feel that a picture is acceptable only if it pleases the teacher, or that ability to draw a recognizable shape is linked with personal worth, i.e., if a child can't draw a good house, she is not clever.

Don't force a child to participate in an art activity

Some children will always want to use the art materials and may spend considerable time doing so. Others are not interested and would rather be involved in the other areas of the room. It is good to give every child the opportunity, but the choice is theirs. Some children may be reluctant because they are afraid they won't know what to do. You may like to suggest that they watch for a while. Or it may be that when other children have finished and they can work at the activity alone they will feel more confident. It does not matter if children do not have a picture to take home. They may have been learning far more in interaction with other children and another teacher in the home area that day.

Occasionally, a child will say 'no' to art during activity time, then be distressed when it is time to go home and he doesn't have a picture. I would usually say, 'Daniel, when I asked you if you wanted to paint, you said no because you were busy with the bricks. You had a good time playing with Mark this morning. Maybe next week you will want to make a picture.' Although a child may be upset, it is part of learning to live with the choices they make. We also need to help parents understand that there is nothing wrong if their child is not particularly interested in art experiences. Many parents feel that their child cannot possibly have learned anything if they didn't 'make a picture'. Sometimes, I deliberately provide an art activity that is not for taking home (like working on a mural

111

together, or fingerpainting with shaving foam) so that none of the children have a picture. This helps the parents to know that we learn in lots of other ways.

This list of guidelines will help you to make the most of any form of art activity, providing experiences that are not only enjoyable, but also valuable times of learning. The types of materials that can be used in art are many and varied. It is not difficult or expensive to provide stimulating opportunities for children to use a host of different materials. Here are several suggestions.

Painting

Painting is probably one of the most universally enjoyed art activities for under fives. There are many different forms of painting, and it can be used over and over without danger of children becoming tired of it. I have used basic easel painting with children as young as eighteen months. With care, painting can even be used in a classroom where children range in age from birth to five. Mixed ages do not deny the children who are old enough the opportunity to use paint.

There are many different ways to use paint:

Easel

With younger children only provide one colour of paint. With three-year-olds and above, make two or more colours available. Thicken powdered paint with flour to make it go further, and always add a small squirt of washing-up liquid to it. This makes it easier to wash out of clothes and off hands. Make only the amount you think you will need for the session — storage of made-up paint is a problem for most churches because of space. You can buy ready-to-use paint, but it can become rather expensive. You can make almost any colour or shade you want from the primary colours (red, yellow and blue) and white. Adding white to any colour makes the shade a pastel.

Chunky brushes are best for easel painting. They are easier for young hands to manage. Always provide some type of smock for covering up clothes. If a child will not wear a smock, then he will not be able to paint. Paint smocks can be made from men's shirts. Cut off the sleeves, and put the shirt on a child so that the buttons are down the back. You can fasten just one button, or clip the shirt together with a clothes peg.

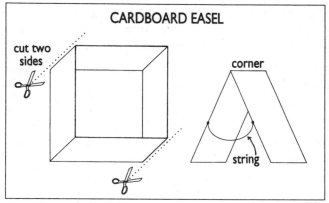

CARDBOARD EASEL

cut two sides

corner

string

The area to be used for painting should be well covered with newspaper or a plastic sheet. If you have an easel, cover it, too, so that you do not have to clean it every time. If you do not have an easel, you can make one from a large, strong cardboard box. Cut out two sides of the box, using the corner as the hinge at the top of the easel. You will need to fix a string, or use a strip of cardboard cut from the rest of the box, as a connecting piece between the two sides of the easel to keep it from collapsing. It can be placed on a low table or used on the floor. Obviously, a cardboard easel won't take much hard wear, but it can be discarded after a few times, and a new one made. Clip the paper to the easel with clothes pegs after writing the child's name on the back.

Show each child how to wipe the brush against the side of the paint container before using it in order to avoid major drips. If the paint is fairly thick it will be easier for the children to use. One child may only put a few marks of paint in the middle of his paper, while another may cover every inch of her paper. Sometimes, for the more enthusiastic painters, it is necessary to give some guidance. 'Nathan, you have put the pretty red paint all over your paper. You may dip the brush one more time, then you will need to finish. Your painting will be too wet to move if you put any more paint on it.' This kind of statement sets a sensible limit without in any way making the child feel that there is anything right or wrong about covering the whole paper. If a child has had a reasonable length of time at the easel and there are other children waiting, you may want to say, 'Kate, you have had a turn to paint now. Anna is waiting for a turn. You may dip your brush two more times, then you will be finished and you may go and do something else.' This gives the child a fair warning that her turn is coming to an end. Sometimes it is helpful to suggest another of the activities that the child might like to participate in.

Sponge

Cut a sponge into one- or two-inch squares. Clip each square to a clothes peg. Put the paint in a shallow container so the children can dip the sponge easily. They will enjoy dabbing the sponge on their paper, or stroking it across the paper as if it were a brush. Any type of painting other than easel painting is best done at a low table or on the floor.

Gadget

Look around your house for various gadgets that can be used for painting. Potato mashers, pastry shapes, empty cotton reels and hair curlers (non-electric, please!) can be used. I find that a rummage round my utensil drawer in the kitchen often yields a few unusual gadgets.

Wheel

Small toy cars, lorries and tractors are fun to paint with. Put the paint in shallow pans so the children can run the wheels through the paint. They can then run them across their paper to make interesting tracks and patterns. Try to find at least one or two cars with some kind of pattern on the wheels, or a tractor with traction on its wheels. If you have remembered to put washing-up liquid in the paint, it usually comes off the cars completely. For this and gadget painting, don't use anything that is precious to anybody, just in case the paint does not wash off very well.

Leaf

Various leaves from trees and bushes make novel 'paint brushes' and give interesting textures.

Golf ball or marble

Use an old shoe box and cut paper to fit inside the box. Put paint into shallow pans and add the golf balls or marbles. Gently spoon the ball or marble into the box. As you tilt the box from side to side, the rolling ball or marble makes an interesting design. Most children really enjoy this type of painting, but may need to be reminded to tilt the box gently rather than shake it up and down!

String

Attach a clothes peg to a twelve-inch piece of string. Dip the string into fairly thin paint. The children can hold the pegs and let the string fall into any pattern they want on their paper. They can either drag the string across the paper, or fold the paper in half with the string on it and draw the string out from inside the folded paper.

Roller bottle

Some types of roll-on deodorant bottles have detachable rollers. When they are empty, they can be filled with paint. Use paint that has been made with water and not thickened with flour. Children will enjoy rolling the paint onto their paper. Provide more than one colour if possible.

Fingerpainting

This can be done using many different substances as paint. Ready-made fingerpaint can be bought, but it is expensive.

Sharing Jesus with under fives

You can make it yourself or use other things to provide the experience. Shaving foam and baby lotion can be squirted directly onto suitable table tops, or onto plastic sheets or trays. Soap flakes mixed with water and beaten with a hand or rotary mixer to the consistency of whipped cream are fun for children to fingerpaint with. You can sprinkle some powdered paint onto the soap mixture as children start to paint to add colour. When they are finished you can place sheets of paper over their paintings and rub until the painting is transferred to the paper.

Fingerpainting is best done standing at a low table or on the floor. This allows for more movement of large muscles. Children need elbow room for fingerpainting. Some children will be straight in with both hands, rubbing paint everywhere, while others will be more unsure, starting with just the tip of one finger. Some children do not enjoy any activity that involves getting their hands messy. For some, this may be because they have been told not to mess their clothes up at church. For others, it is just a function of their personality and nothing lies behind it. If you suspect the former, you may want to have an informal chat to the parents, suggesting that they dress the child in clothes which can be easily washed. You may want to explain that although paint smocks are always used, paint sometimes finds its way onto clothes!

As far as painting is concerned, your imagination is the limit! Obviously, only a few types of painting can be used with toddlers (like easel and roller bottle), but you can use almost anything with older under fives. You may want to change the size, or shape of the paper you provide, sometimes cutting it into circles, triangles or free shapes for variety. Use different colours and shades – pastels in the spring, perhaps, and oranges, browns and yellows in the autumn.

Painting is one of the easiest art activities to provide. You don't need fancy supplies – you don't even have to have brushes! You will, of course need to have a bowl of warm, soapy water and a towel ready for washing hands!

Children love to paint, and it is a prime example of the importance of process, not finished product. I am indebted to my mother for this little poem:

> My painting is yellow, my painting is
>   brown,
> It has little dribbles of paint running
>   down.
> It isn't a house or even a town,
> It's a painting of dribbles of paint running
>   down.

Collage

Like painting, almost anything can be used to make a collage. For younger children, you may want to provide the materials already cut. Older children enjoy using scissors themselves. In a setting of mixed ages, you may want to have some materials ready cut, and others for older children to cut out if they want to. Depending on the theme, you may have pictures of food, people, nature, household goods or animals. Children can choose whatever picture they want, and glue it where they want. Younger ones will need help applying glue, but they can be allowed to glue the picture themselves. Remember, it doesn't matter if it is upside down, or partially covering another picture. It is the conversation you have with them while they are doing it that is important. If you are using the theme, 'God gives us food', you can talk about the kinds of foods they like to eat, what they had for breakfast, or how fruits grow on trees. In this context, it is easy to be natural in saying, 'I'm so glad God gives us different kinds of food to eat. Thank you, God, for food.' When they have finished gluing their pictures of food, you may want to print, 'Thank you, God, for food' on their paper.

Many other things can be used to make collages. Fabric scraps (you will need to cut these), felt shapes, tissue paper, wood shavings, coloured paper scraps and scraps of lace or other trimmings are all suitable. The items used for gluing do not need to have anything to do with the theme for the session. (What does tissue paper have to do with any Bible story?) The activity has value in itself as part of the child's development. Any activity can be turned into a teaching opportunity as we talk to the children while they work. We may talk about colours, shapes and textures, and this will lead to thanking God for eyes and hands. As children share the glue, we may talk about being kind to one another. Every conversation does not have to include words about God. Children are learning much through the relationship they have with their teacher as well as the words she says.

Leaves, twigs, small flowers and stones can be glued onto heavy card to make nature collages. You can collect the items yourself, or if weather and surroundings permit, allow the children to go for a walk and collect items in a box for gluing. As a variation, you may want to give each child a paper bag to collect items, and when he returns to the room, he can glue his items to the bag.

It is common practice to use dried beans, pasta or rice for collage work. Care would need to be exercised to ensure that children do not eat these items. My personal preference is not to use any food items for gluing. There are enough other creative materials available, that I feel it is not necessary to use food items, which some people may view as wasteful. In a world where we must think carefully about distribution of resources and protection of the environment, it is important to set an example, even to young children, of not wasting anything or misusing resources (and this would include toys and equipment).

It is helpful to keep a supply of collage materials ready for use. This saves time hunting around for the right items and then cutting them each time you want to use them. You could use an accordion-type file to store pictures in various categories. Other materials could be stored in bags, all placed in the same box, or in small boxes all fitted in to a larger, shallow box.

Never throw a magazine away without first going through it for suitable pictures. Ask someone you know who knits or sews if they can give you any fabric, wool or trimming scraps. If you have any scraps of coloured paper, or receive any post on coloured paper, cut the blank areas into shapes to add to your paper scraps box. You may be giggling at the images this brings to mind of a scurrying little hoarder, never letting anyone throw anything away! It need not be like that at all. Only save things you know you will use. Try not to become a nag as you remind other family members not to throw magazines away, and sort things out as you go. It only takes a few extra minutes, and saves having piles of magazines and scraps that you intend to 'get around to' one day. Keeping one or two old mail order catalogues around for letting children cut pictures from is useful.

A word about glue. Pritt sticks are clever inventions, but in this setting they tend to get very messy and become very expensive. Buy a bottle of children's glue (a one litre size is about right) and each time you need glue, pour a small amount into a yoghurt pot or an empty film container. Dilute it slightly with water to make it go further. The exception to this is gluing nature items, which are heavier and need full strength glue. You can use plastic glue sticks, small glue brushes or just cotton buds to apply glue to paper. Sometimes it is easier for a child to put the glue on his paper in the place where he wants to stick an item, rather than putting the glue on the item itself. As with painting, have a bowl of warm soapy water available for washing sticky hands.

Collage work can be done on a variety of sizes, shapes and types of paper or card. It can be done as an individual activity, or children can work together on a very large piece of paper to make a collage mural. You may want to display the mural somewhere just outside the classroom so that parents can see it when they come to pick up their children.

Crayons

If you interviewed 100 people at random and asked them to suggest an art activity suitable for use with under fives, most of them would suggest crayons. Crayons can, indeed, be a very useful part of learning through art. They have many things in their favour. But they should not be the only material ever provided for art work.

Crayons are easy to use, require very little preparation beforehand, and are easy to clean up after – no smocks, table coverings or soapy water are necessary! This makes it very tempting to use crayons to the exclusion of other art materials. It may be easier for the teacher, but many potential teaching opportunities may be lost.

What are some of the benefits, as well as drawbacks, of crayons? Using crayons aids the small muscle development of the arms and hands as well as improving eye–hand co-ordination. Making marks with crayons allows children a freedom of expression and the chance to create something that is their own.

A word of caution: most adults naturally link crayons with colouring books or colouring in outlines provided by the teacher. Great care needs to be used here. Children under five can find colouring within an outline very frustrating. Many of them are not physically capable of that level of small muscle control. Asking them to do something they are not capable of is asking them to fail. They may choose, instead, to scribble furiously over the outline. Even those who are able to stay within the lines benefit more, in this setting, from being allowed to create their own drawing. I have nothing against colouring books, *per se*, but I would not want to use them in this teaching context. Secular colouring books usually contain unsuitable pictures for use at church, and most of the 'religious' colouring books have fairly complex drawings that would be far beyond the abilities of the majority of under fives.

Children as young as eighteen months may begin to use chunky crayons. They will, at first, need to be shown how to make a mark with a crayon on a piece of paper. Their random scribblings may appear insignificant to you, but they are the first stage of development in learning to draw. Scribbling is followed by learning to draw shapes, designs, then recognizable pictures. It is not at all unusual for a child to be in the scribbling stage until he is four. Children under three will be perfectly content with several colours of chunky crayons and a large piece of paper.

With children over three you may want, at times, to add variety by the use of rubbings. Any number of items can be used to make texture rubbings with crayons. You may want to use nature items, such as leaves, grasses, tree bark or wood. Sandpaper, netting, corrugated cardboard and coins can be mounted on stiff card to prevent them slipping around when a child puts his paper over them. Many children will need to be shown how to put the crayon on its side and rub it across the paper to make the textured print. In warm weather, you may want to let them take a crayon and paper outside to rub over bricks, textured pavement or tree trunks.

For rubbings, chunky crayons with the papers removed are needed. For ordinary drawing, children over three prefer a slightly slimmer crayon with the paper on and with a reasonable point. These crayons will need to be sharpened before providing them for the children's use. Rather than just having all the crayons mixed together in one box, it might be better to keep two separate boxes of crayons for different purposes. Check it before use to remove any broken crayons and sharpen those that have become dull. It is more inviting to provide a smaller number of crayons (perhaps eight or nine colours) that are in good condition than a large box of old broken fragments.

You may or may not want to provide coloured pencils or washable felt tips. These can add to the expense, and although they are nice, they are not necessary. If it is a choice between buying these or buying paint and brushes, paint would be the wiser choice any time. Most children have easy access to felt tips and pencils at home, but easel and other kinds of painting may be a special treat for them.

The possibilities for the use of art materials are very great. If only the ideas suggested here were used, one each week, they would last for some time. They could then be repeated. In fact, activities such as easel painting can be used as often as once a month without danger of children tiring of them. Remember that one of the ways children learn is through repetition. You may not be excited by the thought of repeating an activity, but they will.

Test all your ideas and practice in art work by the guidelines suggested at the beginning of this section. It takes time to learn the art of teaching through conversation. With experience you will learn how to teach spiritual truth in and relate the Bible to situations arising in the art area of the classroom. At first, you will need to think in advance of the kinds of things you could say to the children as they work. It will sound wooden and clinical to you for a while. But as you persevere, teaching conversation will become more natural to you. You will be amazed at the number of opportunities there are for helping children understand biblical truth in the everyday situations of their lives.

Playdough

Playdough can be used by itself or as part of another activity. It is a versatile medium, but one which can suffer from overuse. I would not recommend having it available every week. From time to time, however, it can be added to another activity area, or used on its own.

Playdough can be used in the home area for the children for pretend cooking, or to roll out as pastry and cut shapes. In the nature area it can be used to make imprints. Stones, leaves or shells can be pressed into it to enable children to see their patterns.

On its own, playdough can be used with children as young as toddlers. I sometimes have some in my bag on Sundays to use at the end of the session while we are waiting for parents to come. I give each child a small ball of dough, and they are happy to roll it around their hands, squeeze it or press their fingers into it. Above the age of two, children enjoy using dough on a hard surface, either a table or a large tray. They may want just to use their hands, but at other times you may want to provide small rolling pins and possibly different shapes for them to cut out. It is probably a good idea to vary the way you use dough, to encourage creativity.

A word of caution about dough: because it is so much fun to play with, the teacher supervising it may find himself rolling a piece around in his hand. The next thing you know, he has made a dog, or some other clever creation. This sets a precedent for some of the children, who may then feel they have to make something recognizable. When they are unable to do this, they either give up playing, or ask the teacher to make one for them. It is then the teacher who is being creative with the dough, not the child. Encourage each child to do what he wishes with the dough. It is not there primarily to 'make things', but for the children to enjoy its texture, and to have the opportunity to use it as they wish. If a child wants his dough rolled out in order to cut shapes, encourage him to try to do it himself. If he is not able to, the teacher may need to help him. If most of the children cannot roll the dough out by themselves, perhaps it is better not to give them rolling pins yet. They may be better just using their hands to squeeze, roll and pound it. Teachers can stimulate ideas and conversation by rolling or squeezing some dough. They need to take care, though, that they do not discourage the children's creativity by dictating what is to be made with the dough.

Playdough recipes

Cooked playdough

1 cup flour	2 tsp. cream of tartar
1 cup water	1 Tbs. cooking oil
½ cup salt	food colouring

In saucepan, mix dry ingredients. NB: the cream of tartar is essential – don't leave it out! Add oil, water, and a few drops of food colouring. Cook for about three minutes or until the mixture pulls away from the sides of the pan. Knead slightly almost immediately.

This is probably the most popular recipe for playdough. It has a nice texture and will keep for some time if stored in an airtight container.

Surprise playdough balls

Prepare playdough. When it is cool, roll it into small balls. Use your finger to poke a hole in each ball down to the centre. Drop two or three drops of food colouring into each ball. Carefully pinch the hole closed on each ball. You may want to make a few balls with each colour of food colouring that you have. As the children play with the dough, they will be delighted to watch it change colours! You can then put each child's dough in a plastic bag for them to take home.

Uncooked playdough

(suitable for making during activity time)
4 cups plain flour
1 cup salt
1½ cups water
food colouring

Blend all ingredients and knead for four or five minutes. This dough has a very granular consistency, and is not really suitable for ongoing use. It is good to use as an activity, though, because it does not require cooking and the children can help.

Chapter 12
Activities

In this section we discuss activities which involve the use of toys: bricks, construction toys and puzzles.

Bricks

Most young children enjoy building with bricks. Bricks provide opportunity for pleasant learning at several levels. On a physical level, stacking, carrying and balancing require the use of different muscles and develop eye–hand co-ordination. Two or more children playing with bricks at the same time allows for social interaction. For toddlers and two-year-olds, playing side by side (parallel play) is the forerunner to playing with another child. For three- to five-year-olds, there are opportunities for sharing, working together and imaginative play. A child playing alone with bricks can develop his own imagination and gain a sense of satisfaction at what he builds.

Even babies can benefit from brick activity. As they hold a large brick, or lay on the floor and push it around, they are taking the first step towards playing when they can sit alone. As a baby watches, a teacher can stack two or three bricks, saying 'up' and then gently knocking them over, saying 'down'. The teacher may then say, 'John can see the bricks. Thank you, God, for John's eyes'.

As a child begins to crawl and walk, he may enjoy playing with large bricks that he can move around. From around the age of two, he will begin to stack and build more creatively with wooden building bricks. As he gets older, more and different shapes can be added to the bricks.

It is helpful to have some guidelines for the use of the bricks. Some principles that may be useful are:
● Play with the bricks on the floor, not chairs and tables
● Bricks are for building rather than throwing or kicking

- Build no higher than your chin – this would apply to smaller bricks when seated and larger bricks when standing
- Take brick 'creations' down brick by brick, rather than knocking them over
- Keep the bricks in the brick area – this area may be defined by a piece of carpet that the bricks stay on, or by putting tape on the floor to outline the boundaries.

Some children may have to be reminded many times before they learn these guidelines!

Different 'accessories' may be added to the bricks each week in keeping with the theme for the day. For instance, wooden or plastic animals may be added to enforce the teaching that God made the animals. Stand-up figures can be made by cutting out pictures of people or animals, mounting them on lightweight card and then attaching them to the appropriate sized piece of cardboard tubing (empty loo rolls!). Remember that these pictures or wooden figures need to be life-like. Cartoon characters and animals wearing clothes or driving cars are not realistic and may cause the child to confuse that fantasy with biblical reality.

Masking tape can be put on the floor or carpet to make roads for towns. Twigs and flowers can be stuck into lumps of playdough to make trees. Sometimes, just a picture that illustrates the Bible story or some aspect of the theme can be mounted on card and placed with the bricks to prompt conversations.

If the Bible story is about the friendship between David and Jonathan, a modern picture of friends can lead to several conversations with different children. You may talk about the picture, then ask a child, 'Who are your friends?' You may tell a few lines of the story or say, 'Today we have a story from the Bible about two boys who were very good friends. Mark, you and Sarah are playing together. You are friends. Thank you, God, for friends.' You may sing a song to a few children playing together:

It's fun to play with friends at church,
   friends at church, friends at church.
It's fun to play with friends at church,
   thank you, God, for my friends.

(To the tune of
'Here we go round the mulberry bush'.)

Accessories are not always necessary, but can be added for one session in order to make additional teaching opportunities. They also stimulate new interest amongst the children.

What kind of bricks are best to use? For babies and toddlers, large bricks are good for encouraging movement of large muscle groups. You can purchase big plastic bricks, but choose carefully – some of them have rather sharp corners. You can easily make cardboard bricks by saving milk cartons and boxes of various sizes when cooking. Stuff them full of newspaper wads and then seal them with tape. Cover them with coloured sticky-backed plastic, and you have a set of bricks for only the time and the cost of a roll of plastic contact paper.

Two-year-olds and above generally use wooden bricks more creatively. Again, these can be purchased at most toy stores or the Early Learning Centre. Make sure they are not too small, as younger children may be tempted to put them in their mouths. Also, smaller bricks get lost easily, and are harder for young hands to build with. Wooden bricks can be expensive, but if you are going to buy them, it is better to invest in a good set than buy a cheaper set which may splinter. It is not necessary for the bricks to be painted. Natural wood colour is fine. A good set of bricks carefully looked after will last for years.

You can, of course, make wooden bricks by obtaining suitable wood from a lumber yard and securing the time and help of someone with the right tools and know-how! Some lumber yards may be happy to give you scraps of wood for nothing if you tell them why you want them. The

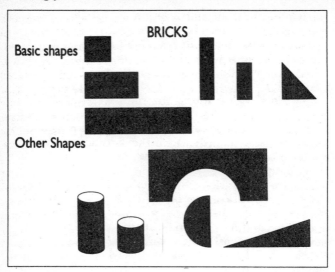

bricks do not need to be painted. A good smooth sanding and possibly a coat of suitable varnish will make a super set of bricks. A variety of shapes and sizes make the bricks more interesting – squares, rectangles and triangles are sufficient. For the more competent woodworker, cylinders, ramps and half-circles are very useful.

Bricks provide an interesting, multi-use teaching tool for the under fives. Playing with bricks is fun for the children, allows time for social interaction and creates many opportunities for learning through conversation and music.

Construction toys

There are a number of construction toys available that can be used in addition to bricks. These would not be appropriate for babies, but for toddlers and up they can create new interest.

Toddlers may enjoy building with large pieces like Duplo, or its equivalent. Make sure the pieces are large enough not to be swallowed. At this age, the 'novelty' pieces are not necessary. If you have some of the ones that rattle or have wheels, that is fine. If you only have the basic stacking squares and rectangles, don't worry, they are adequate. Three- and four-year-olds may enjoy some of the pieces that allow them to make trains and bridges, but if you do not have these, it does not matter. Avoid the pieces that would encourage unhelpful play, such as pirates. You may want to use Duplo instead of bricks one week, but it can be used in addition to them as well. Some children will still prefer ordinary wooden bricks. This is particularly true of toddlers and two-year-olds, who may not yet have the dexterity necessary for Duplo.

(N.B. Although Lego is an extremely popular building toy, using it at church can be very impractical. Many of the pieces are so small they are easily lost. Small hands find these tiny pieces difficult to manage, and this can lead to frustration. In a room that has mixed ages, Lego would be dangerous – babies may swallow it, and toddlers may throw it around. It is perhaps best left for use at home.)

Two-year-olds and above enjoy Stickle Bricks. These are colourful and durable. They can be stuck together just for fun, or can be built into almost anything.

Three- and four-year-olds like to play with Construct-O-Straws, Octons and other building toys. There are many variations on this theme. It is not necessary to go out and buy them. You can teach successfully without them. But if you have access to them, either from your own toyshelf at home or from other families in the church, you may find them useful. Sometimes you find second-hand sets of these items at car boot sales. If they are in good condition and at a reasonable price, you may want to buy them. Make sure you wash them before you use them.

A practical way to store construction toys is in cloth drawstring bags. Someone who sews may be able to make some for you from left-over pieces of fabric. They are easy to transport this way, and easy for children to put away. One child holds the bag, the others put the bricks in. Cloth bags are durable, washable, and can be stored by hanging from nails or strong hooks on the wall.

Puzzles

Puzzles are far more than just wooden or cardboard frames with a number of pieces that fit in a specific way to complete the picture. Puzzles can be defined as any materials which present a difficulty that needs to be solved. Any activity that requires a child to match colours, shapes or pictures, put certain things into certain spaces, or fit two or more items together by manipulation or trial and error could be described as a puzzle.

Puzzles are valuable for use with under fives because they represent problem-solving activities. The simple skills acquired by working puzzles in this context lay foundations for other, more demanding problem solving as the child grows. All the things we have mentioned about eye–hand co-ordination and development of small muscle control apply to puzzles. Opportunities for social interaction and conversational teaching are also available through the use of puzzles.

In addition, puzzles are intriguing and present a challenge to children. If the level of difficulty is appropriate to their stage of development, it is a challenge they will rise to. They will usually want to finish it by themselves. With more difficult puzzles, children may be encouraged to work together and help each other. Even when help from a teacher is required, a child can still have some sense of satisfaction when they look at the completed task.

There are many different types of puzzle activities, most of which you can make, or buy very inexpensively. Let's look at some ideas.

Conventional puzzles

We will start with the exception to the low-cost rule. Good wooden puzzles are expensive to buy, but are generally a worthwhile long-term investment. If they are carefully looked after, and pieces always accounted for at the end of every session, they last for many years. Because of the need to use realistic, non-fictional characters and pictures, suitable wooden puzzles are hard to find. Appropriate farm scenes and transport pictures are the ones you are most likely to see. Sometimes you find good pictures on cardboard puzzles. These are less expensive than wooden ones, but will not be as durable. With careful use, though, cardboard puzzles can last for a few years.

Children enjoy working conventional puzzles over and over again. If you can provide some for the children's use, they will, no doubt, prove popular. If you have half a dozen, it is better to put out only three each week, and not always in the same combination. You may want to help the children understand some guidelines for their use:

- If a child starts a puzzle, they need to finish it before they move on to something else. This helps to teach children responsibility. It also avoids having pieces from various puzzles scattered across the table or the floor area. Assure the child that if they need assistance, they will receive it. You may want to help them yourself, or in a room with mixed ages, ask an older pre-schooler to help.
- Puzzles are to be kept in the puzzle area, or if you have a shelf where they are stored, they should be returned to the shelf when a child is finished with them.
- Older under fives can be encouraged to remove the pieces one at a time, rather than turning the puzzle over and dumping them out.

If conventional puzzles are outside your budget, do not worry. There are many puzzle activities you can make with a minimum of time and expense. The children will enjoy these just as much. In fact, sometimes they are more interested in a home-made puzzle, because they have never seen one quite like it before.

Stacking and nesting puzzles

This type of puzzle activity can be used even with babies. You may be able to buy a set of nesting/stacking beakers. You may need to remove the smallest one or two to prevent them being swallowed. As you show a baby how to nest them or stack them, they become aware that only certain ones will fit inside certain others. Although they will not

131

yet be able to arrange them according to size, they will begin to understand the concept. You can say, 'Thank you, God, for Matthew's eyes to see the beakers.' As you observe a baby handling and exploring the toy, you could say, 'You are holding the beakers in your hands to look at them. Thank you, God, for Hannah's hands.'

You can make nesting/stacking puzzles from different sizes of small cardboard boxes, various plastic containers or even metal cans. You may want to glue a piece of felt into the bottom of each can to reduce the noise when one is dropped into another! Of course, you will want to make sure that all edges are safe and smooth. It may make the rims of cans safer if you cover them with heavy tape. You can use boxes as they are, or if you want to make them more uniform, you could cover each one with a different colour of sticky-backed plastic. This will involve the price of the plastic, though, and may defeat your attempts to save money. You could just as easily colour them with crayons or felt tips, or paint them.

Simple nesting toys can be used with babies as soon as they are able to hold an object. Even three- and four-year-olds can enjoy more difficult nesting puzzles. Because home-made ones will have non-uniform pieces, they present an interesting challenge to an older child. They may have to work to decide whether a flat can, such as the size used for tuna or salmon, fits into a taller can, or the other way around.

Perhaps you have not thought of stacking/nesting toys, bought or home-made, as puzzles. But they present difficulties to be solved and involve fitting two or more objects together. So they are not just toys, they represent teaching opportunities.

Shape sorters

Again, there are a wide variety of shape sorting puzzles available in most toy stores. Although some have too many pieces, are too complicated or have inappropriate pictures on them, many are brightly coloured and simple in design. They range from as few as six pieces (two each of three shapes) through to as many as twenty pieces, with ten shapes. The very simple ones can be used with toddlers, and even four-year-olds will enjoy some of the more complicated ones. Most of them are very durable, so as long as you keep track of all the pieces, they last a long time.

There are other ways to give the children shape sorting puzzles without having to spend a lot of money. For older babies and toddlers, you can use a strong shoe box with a lid to make a simple sorter. Purchase a few small balls, such as table tennis balls. Cut a hole in the lid of the box big enough for the balls to go through. The children will enjoy putting the balls into the box, then emptying them and doing it again. The large tins that powdered baby milk comes in are also good for this. You can cut a hole in the plastic lid. The balls make a nice sound as they drop onto the metal of the can. If the noise is a problem, you could glue a piece of felt in the bottom to muffle it. Interestingly, as children learn to put the right shapes in holes, almost all of them learn a round shape first. I have observed many toddlers using a three shape sorter, and they always put the round shapes in first. Fitting a square or triangle in is more difficult, because of the corners and angles. You can increase the difficulty of the puzzle for older children by cutting holes for other shapes, perhaps using triangles, squares and rectangles from a set of wooden bricks.

Even before a toddler can put a specific shape into a specific hole, he will enjoy putting items into a container and then emptying them out. You could call this a 'fill and dump' toy. The tall, plastic jars that sweets come in are great for this. Most sweet shops are happy to sell them to you for only a few pence. Any number of items can be dropped into the wide opening at the top, then tipped out again. You could use small balls (not small enough to choke on), clothes pegs, old hair curlers, small jar lids – almost anything can be used as long as it is the right size and unbreakable. I find that a set of snapping beads is good for this. They are brightly coloured, a good size for small hands but again, not too small to put in the mouth, and a set of sixteen just fills the plastic jar. Some of the older babies enjoy just putting them in and dumping them out. The older toddlers like to snap the beads together and then take them apart. Snapping beads are inexpensive, and are a good buy for babies and toddlers because they can be used in different ways.

Matching and sorting puzzles

In this category, the possibilities are endless. A little time and creativity can produce endless varieties of puzzle activities. You will need to adjust the ideas to suit the age group you are teaching, but most of them are fairly adaptable.

One of the easiest types of sorting is by colour. Younger children may be able to sort clothes pegs by colour. Provide three colours of plastic clothes pegs, and three containers. Put a different coloured peg into each container and help a toddler sort out the rest. For this age, you will only need about three or four pegs of each colour. The same idea can be adapted for older children, using more colours. If plastic pegs of several colours are not available, paint wooden ones or colour them with felt tips. Two or three pegs in each of six or eight colours would be appropriate for older three- and four-year-olds. On the edges of a small cardboard box (a shoe box works well) colour or paint a section in each of the colours. Place the pegs in the box. The children can peg them to the appropriate colour section of the edge of the box.

As you get used to the abilities of different age groups, you will learn to judge the difficulty level of the puzzles you make. Even after many years, I still sometimes misjudge. On Sunday I made the clothes peg and box puzzle for my class of toddlers, who range in age from 15 months to 2½ years. I chose four bright colours – red, yellow, blue and green – thinking that they would be able to manage that visually. What I had not thought of was what they could manage physically – they were not able to open the pegs to put them on the edge of the box! So much for that idea! One enterprising two-year-old did manage to find a way to make it work. She rested the pegs on the edge of the box upside down so that she did not have to squeeze them open!

Other possibilities for colour sorting might be:

- *sorting out pairs of socks* Provide a variety of colours, patterns and sizes of socks for the children to match up. If you don't have such a variety yourself, ask a young family in the church with children of various ages. They are bound to have quite a range of sizes and colours and would probably be quite happy to loan them to you for a morning!

- *sorting out mittens and gloves* This is the same principle as above. Alternatively, you could cut out a mitten shape from construction paper. Cut a pair of mittens in a number of different colours and let the children match them up.

- *coloured paper shapes* Cut out a variety of shapes in several different colours. These can be sorted out by colour or by shape. You could also cut several colours of just one shape, a fish, a flower, a star, or any other simple shape.

- *button sorting* Older children love to play with buttons but again be careful with younger children. Someone in your church who sews or knits a lot may well have a 'button box'. Choose several buttons in each of several colours, including gold or silver, or even wooden buttons. If you choose six different colours they can be neatly sorted into the compartments of an egg carton.

In each of these puzzle activities you would vary the number of colours according to the age of the children. For two-year-olds, three or four colours are sufficient. The primary colours (red, yellow and blue) are the ones they will most easily recognize. Four-year-olds can work with up to eight colours. As with many of the activities, teaching occurs through interaction and conversation. As children sort the colours you may tell them two or three sentences of the Bible story. You may be able to use a Bible verse with them. As they sort coloured flower shapes you may talk with them about flowers they see in gardens. You may even have a vase of brightly coloured flowers on the table with the shapes. This can lead to thanking God for eyes to see, or for the beauty of his creation. In the section where we look at how to use the Bible you will find more clues about how to guide conversation and use it positively. At first, you will find that it seems contrived and calculated, but the more you do it, the more natural it will become.

There are numerous other ideas for matching and sorting puzzles. Here are a few that I have tried:

- *wallpaper* Obtain an outdated wallpaper sample book, or even just several pages from one. Cut various shapes from each page, leaving the surrounding paper intact. The children can fit the shape and colour or pattern into the appropriate 'frame'. If you want to make these puzzles more durable, you could cover both sides of the sheet of wallpaper with clear sticky-backed plastic before you cut out the shapes. Alternatively, you could mount the sheet onto thin cardboard before cutting. For two-year-olds you might want to cut the sheet of wallpaper so that it fits into a shallow box lid, like the lid of a shoe box. If you glue it into the lid, the children may find it easier to put the three or four shapes into it. For older children you can mix the sheets and shapes together so that they can sort out not only shape, but pattern as well.
- *car pictures* Ask a car dealer for two identical brochures about cars. Cut out pictures of various types and colours of cars. Mount one complete set on a large piece of card. The children can then match up the other set by laying them on top of the corresponding picture. Again, durability can be increased by covering pictures or mounting them on card.
- *clothes and seasons* From a mail order catalogue, cut out pictures of clothes and accessories which would be used in various types of weather – hot, cold, and rainy, for instance. Either draw or cut out a picture demonstrating each of these types of weather. Let the children match

the clothes to the appropriate weather. This provides many opportunities for fun conversation not only about what we wear, but what we do in different types of weather. Alternatively, provide real clothes – coats, wellington boots, sandals, shorts, sun hats, etc. The children may want to try some of them on as they match them to different types of weather.

The idea for the wallpaper puzzles could also be used with coloured construction paper, coloured card or even fabric, which would, of course, need to be mounted. The car puzzle idea could be used with any other matching sets of pictures you can obtain – food, houses or nature items would be suitable.

Picture puzzles

You can make your own fit-together picture puzzles. From catering companies or college catering courses you can obtain old brochures with some wonderful pictures of food. Choose pictures that are at least five by seven inches. Mount them on thin card and then on the back draw lines for cutting them into puzzles. Vary the number of pieces and the difficulty with which they fit together according to the age you are teaching. If you can cut them to fit inside a shallow box lid 'frame', they will be suitable for use with younger children. If they have no framework, they can be used with older threes and four-year-olds.

This same principle applies to making any picture puzzle. Nature scenes, pictures of people either on their own or with others and pictures of animals would all be appropriate.

Threading spools and beads

This activity comes under the heading of puzzles because it presents a difficulty to be solved, certain things that must be fitted together in certain ways. This task is more appropriate for age three and up. Two-year-olds might manage it, but they require a great deal of help, and may become frustrated if they cannot do it. You can purchase plastic reels for threading, or you can ask seamstresses to save them for you. You can use them as they are or you can paint them bright colours. They can be threaded on to a shoelace or a piece of smooth chunky wool. To make a hard end for threading, either dip the end into clear nail varnish, or wrap it around with sellotape.

As you begin to make puzzles for use with under fives many other ideas may come to you. If you choose to make more durable puzzles that can be used again you will need some organized, safe way of storing them. Even with home-made puzzles, always check that all the pieces are there as you tidy up after a session. A puzzle is no good to a child when there is a piece missing.

If you have more than one teacher in a room, you can provide some kind of puzzle activity each week. Sometimes it will be linked to the theme for the day. Other times, it will be a puzzle just for the benefit of a puzzle.

Chapter 13
Books and pictures

Books

'Read it again!' is a plea often heard from young children. Because they learn through repetition, they can have a book read to them dozens of times before they tire of it. Even when they seem to have memorized every page (and they notice if you miss out even one word!) they may still bring it to you time and time again.

Reading or looking at books can be a very beneficial experience for both teacher and child. Children who have the opportunity to handle books from a very early age often show a greater keenness for learning to read. When babies see familiar objects in picture books, and hear a teacher say the name of the object, it reinforces their knowledge about that object. As they see pictures of unfamiliar objects, or of animals, they hear new words as a teacher names each picture. Toddlers and two-year-olds begin to be able to listen to short sentences on each page of a book, or to name objects (and make appropriate sounds!) themselves. A child's readiness to listen to stories, as opposed to 'picture reading', varies with his developmental stage, and sometimes with his vocabulary. Some children can listen to a story in a book for five minutes even at just two years of age. Other children, who may be three or four, seem unable to concentrate for more than a minute or two. Books must be used with each child according to their readiness and level of interest.

Books are not only useful in terms of mental growth, but they are of social and emotional benefit, as well. As a teacher sits on the floor with a book, a child may come and snuggle up next to him, or sit on his lap. This one-on-one time can be very valuable. Sometimes two or three children may sit with a teacher to look at a book. They may take turns turning over the pages, or naming various objects.

In a room of mixed ages, a four-year-old may 'read' a book to a younger child. Sharing books in any of these ways can be both enjoyable and enriching.

Books can be used in an area by themselves, or in conjunction with another activity area. If, for instance, a doctor's kit has been added to the home area, a book about a child going to the doctor, or being in hospital may be placed with the other items. As a teacher looks at the book with one or more children, there may be opportunities for them to talk about when they have visited the doctor's surgery or have been in hospital. If the emphasis in the brick area is on construction, a book about a new house or building being built might be of interest to the children.

It is often useful to provide a quiet corner or area just for looking at books, if possible. If this can happen every week, a child can go to that place to be quiet, or to be alone. If a book area can only be offered occasionally, perhaps you could ask another adult to come in and sit in that area for the express purpose of being available to read. A few pillows or cushions on the floor, or a special blanket, will clearly designate the area. In a busy classroom it is difficult for a teacher to sit for very long and read with children. Having someone come in for that purpose alone will be a special treat for some children.

The types of books that will be appropriate will vary, of course, with the different age groups. For babies and young toddlers, plastic books, or the ones made of heavy card ('board books') are best. Children of this age will not only look at books, they will taste them as well! Also, paper pages are difficult for tiny hands, and get torn too easily. Some two-year-olds can manage to turn paper pages, and most three- and four-year-olds are accustomed to handling books. (Even those who come from homes where books are not readily available will probably have used books at playgroup or nursery school.) From the earliest age, children can be taught to look after books properly. A toddler can be reminded not to stand on a book or kick it. Two- and three-year-olds can be helped to turn pages gently and carefully, and taught that folding books back damages the binding.

What about the length of books? For babies, picture books with no words, or only one or two words on a page are suitable. A young baby can focus on a picture in a book, particularly if it is brightly coloured. Pictures that are realistic and clearly drawn are best. Pictures of objects and scenes that are familiar to them will help them connect words and images they have already seen. Toddlers and two-year-olds begin to manage a sentence or two on a page. As their vocabulary expands and they begin to put words together, they are helped by having books with simple sentences. Again, lots of bright pictures will grab their interest. Three- and four-year-olds will benefit most from books that are short enough to be finished in one sitting. At home they may be able to sit for several minutes and listen to a story. At church, with other children around, and lots of other activity, their concentration may be less intense, and not last as long.

As important as the visual impact of books is for children, in this context content is crucial. There are many beautifully produced books, with bright pictures, and just the right number of words. They may, however, not be appropriate for use at church. I am all in favour of *Postman Pat*, *Thomas the Tank Engine* and *Fireman Sam*, but I would rather not use them at church. Also, there are some lovely books that feature various endearing animals and their escapades in the woodland, but they are not suitable either. In these stories, the animals talk to one another, and in other ways behave like humans.

At this point you may be thinking one of two things. You may be feeling condemned, worrying that you have stunted the spiritual growth of the children in your church because you have provided them with fairy tales and *Winnie the Pooh* stories. This is not the case. Remember that we are talking about various learning activities in terms of the best possible situations. Very few of us can operate with the best materials and the best equipment all of the time. Even if we could, *we* may not be at our best each week, so perfection is never attained. The material in this book will, I hope, be a guideline, and a goal at which to aim, not a strait-jacket from which you squirm to escape. You may have read many things in these chapters which are different from what you have been doing. Rather than feeling condemned, think through each idea. If you agree with it, work towards implementing it. If you don't agree, then at least you will be confident that you have thought through the issues.

The other thing you may be thinking is that if all the books we have described are unsuitable, what else is left?! Despite the seemingly large number of factors that disqualify a book, there are plenty left. Look carefully at your nearest Christian book-shop. Even there, some of the books will not be the best for under fives, but you will find many that you can use with the various age groups. Secular publishers produce many books which you can use. Some of the picture books for babies have either photographs or very realistic drawings of everyday objects. Many animal books are full of beautiful photos of animals in their natural habitat. Books about farms are often very accurate. For older pre-schoolers, you will find books dealing with specific issues such as hospitalization, a new baby in the family or moving house.

As well as suitability, the other difficulty in acquiring books is cost. Good books are expensive. If you do buy books, make your purchases very carefully, trying to choose books with a wide appeal. There are other ways of building up your book collection for use with under fives. Families in the church whose children are all now in school may be willing to let you check through their books to see if any might be useful. You may be able to borrow books for a short time from some of the families with young children. Your local library could be an invaluable source of books, providing you with a huge selection and variety.

Sometimes you may want to make a book. I keep an old photograph album for this purpose. It is one of those with the clear sheet that sticks to the page, which you can use over and over. I change the pictures to fit the theme. One week it held a picture of a different food on each page. Another week I cut out pictures of things to do with water, such as a boat, an umbrella, someone swimming, someone having a bath, and so on. If I don't have a book in my collection that fits the theme, I may try to make one.

Three- and four-year-olds may enjoy making a book themselves. They can either cut out pictures to fit the theme, or draw their own. They may want to tell you about their picture and you can write it on their page of the book. After all the children who want to have participated, punch holes in the papers, and tie them together with ribbon or wool. You can use the book at group time. I remember a few years ago when the theme dealt with families. I provided some pieces of paper for the children to draw something they like to do with their family or with someone in their family. They then told me about it, and I wrote on each page. So one page said, 'Kathryn likes to play in the garden with her Daddy'. Another page said, 'Edward shares a bedroom with his little sister'. At group time when we read the book, the children were thrilled to hear their names read out. Even when we have just made books about food by cutting and pasting pictures, they are always keen to say, 'That's the picture I glued!'.

One time we made a very special book by taking pictures of the children with a Polaroid camera. We took them in groups of three in order to use the expensive film sparingly. Just watching the pictures develop before their eyes was exciting for them. We put each picture on a page and wrote, 'Jesus loves —, — and —', inserting each child's name. They were then allowed to draw on their page if they wanted to. We put this book out for several weeks in a row. It eventually found its way to the bottom of one of my boxes, and I found it about a year later. How interesting it was to see how much they had all changed!

The Bible is the most special book of all, and it should be available every week. We will look at how to use it in the section entitled, 'Using the Bible'.

Books are a useful teaching tool, whether you can

provide them every week, or just occasionally, to illustrate a particular theme. Even if you cannot purchase books for use at church, think creatively about other ways to make books available. Sharing a book with a child can be a special relationship builder. Books can arouse curiosity and stimulate learning. As we give young children a love for books, they will be more ready to grow up with a love for the most important book – the Bible.

Pictures

'A picture is worth a thousand words' is a saying we have all heard at some time or other. Photos of happy holidays we have enjoyed are nice to look at even years after the event. Pictures of things and places we have never seen help us to understand more clearly. Someone may try to describe to us a particular scene. We may listen carefully, but if they can show us a picture, we can visualize what their words have tried to convey. Pictures are useful and valuable to us as adults. How much more so for children!

A toddler may bring you a book to 'read'. What he might actually mean is look at the pictures. Young children find it hard to listen to a book when there aren't any pictures to look at. Pictures can help children understand things more clearly. They enjoy seeing pictures of familiar objects, and of children doing things they have done. Pictures that depict happy scenes can elicit warm emotional responses from children. Factual pictures of events like visiting the doctor or the hospital can provoke conversation that helps children have more positive attitudes or overcome fears.

You can teach through pictures whether you use them as a separate activity, or integrate them into all the other activity areas you use. Like music, they are very versatile, and can be used effectively in almost any situation.

Over time you can build up a file of pictures that can be used repeatedly. If you mount them carefully, they will last much longer. When you come across a good picture, hang on to it. Appropriate pictures are not always easy to find.

Some characteristics of an appropriate teaching picture would be:

- Realistic, not abstract or fantasy
- Clear, with an uncluttered background
- Uncomplicated – easy for the child to see what you want them to see
- Large enough to be shown to several children at the same time – 6×8 inches would be the smallest size you could use this way
- Small enough for a child to hold – big posters are nice, but children like not only to see pictures, but to touch them as well.

Pictures containing familiar objects, food, pets, animals, weather, families, people involved in familiar activities, houses and furniture are all useful. Children enjoy seeing pictures of workers they see in the community – the postman, the milkman, policemen, firemen and doctors and nurses are examples.

These types of pictures take some looking for. It is best to always have your eyes open for such scenes. Old magazines, copies of *National Geographic*, even old books that are beyond repair may be sources for pictures. Someone you know may have taken some excellent photographs of animals or people, and they may be happy to give you the negatives so you can have them enlarged. Old picture calendars, gardening catalogues and various colour brochures may also have suitable pictures.

If you want a picture for a specific theme, you may look in dozens of places and not find one. The very next week you may come across two pictures that would be perfect. That is the nature of things. Keep the pictures anyway – you may want to use them again sometime.

Some pictures are so good they are worth mounting for long term use. Cut a piece of thick cardboard (corrugated cardboard is good for this purpose) exactly the size of the picture. Cut a piece of clear, sticky-backed plastic about two inches larger than the picture on all four sides. If the picture does not have straight edges, you may want to glue it on to a rectangular piece of plain or coloured paper before mounting it on to the cardboard. Lay the plastic flat on the table, sticky side up. Carefully lay the picture on it, face

145

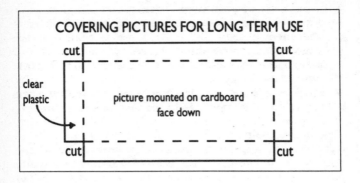

COVERING PICTURES FOR LONG TERM USE

cut   cut

clear plastic

picture mounted on cardboard face down

cut   cut

down. Put the cardboard on top of the picture and hold it steady. Cut the corners of the plastic to ensure even folding, then fold each edge up over the cardboard and press it down smoothly. Sticky-backed plastic is hard to work with at first, but you soon get a feel for it.

You may want to use pictures of animals or of the natural world with a nature activity you are providing. If you are bringing in different types of leaves, you may want to prop up a picture of some trees next to them. A picture of a squirrel or of a bird's nest in a tree might also be appropriate.

If you have added adult dress-up clothes to the home area, you may want to have one or two pictures of adults doing various things – working in the office, cleaning the house or car, or interacting with children.

On a day when you have provided home-made musical instruments or invited a guest with an instrument to visit, pictures of a variety of other instruments might be useful. Children may have seen a piano, a violin or a trumpet. If they are listening to a recording of instrumental music, they may be interested to see pictures of the specific instrument playing at any one time. (A catalogue from a music store might be a good source for such pictures.)

The pictures you use on these occasions may well be used

again. You will probably not want to mount and cover all your pictures, but you might at least want to glue them onto a piece of heavy paper or thin card. As with pictures for collage an accordion file with several sections is useful for categorizing and storing pictures.

You can use simple, clear pictures with young babies. Show them a picture as they sit on your lap. As a baby lays in her carry cot, show her a picture of a bird. You can talk to her about the picture. 'Christina, this is a bird. We can hear the birds sing. We can see them fly in the sky. Thank you, God, for birds.'

Another way to give babies the opportunity to see pictures is to make a picture cube. Take an empty tissue box (the tall kind, not the flatter ones), and stuff it full of newspaper. Cover it with coloured construction paper. On each of the six sides, glue a picture – you may have six pictures of flowers, or of different animals. Cover the whole cube with sticky-backed plastic. As a baby lays on the floor on her stomach she can look at it and push it around. As she sits up, she can hold it in her hands and turn it around to see all the pictures. You can talk to her and sing about the pictures as she plays.

Pictures are best used for a particular reason on a given week, then put away for another time. If you leave the same pictures out every time, children grow used to them, and no longer 'see' them. If you are using a similar theme two weeks in a row, the same picture might apply. If the children enjoyed seeing it, they may be glad to look at it again the next week. After that, it should be put away until it is next appropriate.

Here are a few ideas if you want to use pictures as an activity in and of themselves:

People pictures

Cut out several pictures of people of various ages – a baby, a toddler, a child of school age, a teenager, an adult, and an older person. Make a set of a male, and a set of a female. See if the children can place the pictures in the right order. As they do this, you can talk with them about the different

147

things people are able to do at each age. Talk with them about the way God planned for us to grow. (This activity could also be described as a puzzle.)

'Hide' various pictures around the room

For toddlers and two-year-olds these may be pictures of animals or everyday objects. For three- and four-year-olds you could use these, or more complicated pictures, such as pictures of people involved in various activities. Young children may just want to find the pictures and bring them to you to look at and talk about. Older under fives may like it if you give them a specific picture to find. 'Mark, can you find a picture of two friends playing together while Susan finds a picture of someone cooking?'

Matching/Pairing pictures

Obtain several pictures that match in some way. Mother animals and their babies are a good example. Pictures of clothing that correspond to various activities, like a picture of pyjamas and a picture of a bed, an umbrella or wellies and a picture of rain would also be appropriate for four-year-olds. Mix the pictures together and see if the children can match them up. If a child matches incorrectly, ask him why he put two pictures together. He may operate on a completely different thought pattern from you. This does not mean he is wrong. You may learn something from him. For instance, if he matches wellies with a bed, it may be that he stores his wellies underneath his bed!

Holiday postcards and photographs

In the summertime, you may want to provide several postcards from various holiday places, and a few brochures from a travel agent. You could ask the parents a few weeks in advance for one or two photos from past family holidays. Bring an empty photo album to put them in, and include one or two photos of yourself on holiday. Children love to look at pictures of themselves and other children in the class. Return the photos to the parents at the end of the session as they collect their children. (This idea works very well for a family theme, or a growing up theme. Children can bring in pictures of their families, or of themselves as babies.)

Bible story pictures

Pictures that illustrate Bible stories are good to use with all ages under five. Children who are not old enough to have group time can still hear a Bible story. The teacher may tell it in a few short sentences at various times throughout the session. The story is reinforced if they can see a picture. Children who are old enough for group time enjoy seeing a picture after they have heard the story.

Bible story pictures that meet the criteria suggested at the beginning of this section are hard to find. Many of the pictures from older books reflect the era in which they were used. Biblical characters are drawn with beatific smiles and halos of light around their heads. Although these pictures may seem funny to us now, children don't always notice these things. Some of these pictures, carefully chosen, can still be used.

The tendency in recent years has been to make the pictures more like cartoon pictures. This is not very helpful, either, as the pictures do not look realistic. Some of them may be useful, but some are better left. Although it is helpful to have a picture to show children, it is not essential. It is probably better to have no picture, than to have a picture that gives them the wrong idea.

The other difficulty with Bible story pictures is that many of them illustrate stories that are not particularly appropriate for use with under fives. We will look at that issue in the section on 'Using the Bible'.

We may be limited in our use of biblical pictures with under fives, but there is a great variety of other pictures we can use. Let's make the most of those, both in conjunction with other activities, and as an activity in and of themselves. If a picture *is* worth a thousand words, then proper use of pictures will save us a lot of talking!

Chapter 14

Home corner

Purpose

Many an interesting conversation has been heard as children play in the home area! This is the part of the room that is arranged to enable children to pretend the thing they are most familiar with — life at home. Children learn a great deal as they act out the roles of various family members and copy the activities related to work in the home. They are involved physically, mentally and socially as they use the home area.

A teacher can learn much about a child by listening to his conversation and watching his actions in the home area. Interaction with children in the home area is enriched as a teacher knows more about each child's family situation. If a four-year-old is playing very roughly with the doll, a teacher may be helped to talk with the child more meaningfully if aware that a new baby has recently come into the family. The child may be acting out resentment towards the new baby for taking so much of Mum and Dad's time.

A three-year-old who is playing 'mums and dads' with one or two other children may be openly affectionate in giving hugs. This may reveal that he comes from a home where love is easily and readily expressed through physical touch. The teacher may want to help that child relate his happy experiences at home to God's care for families by saying, 'Thank you, God, for mums and dads who love us'.

Because the home area contains items that are familiar to the children it may be a part of the room that makes them feel secure. Some children will spend most of any session in the home area. Others may go there first, then look around and see what other activities are being offered. The home area needs to be easily accessible to children *and* teachers. 'Wendy Houses' are great fun for children, but are probably not appropriate in this setting because they make it difficult for the teacher to see or hear what is going on inside them. They preclude teacher involvement as well – not many adults can easily sit comfortably in such a small space, and still leave room for the children!

The home area, like the brick area, should be a designated part of the room. Its boundaries can be noted by the way the home area materials are arranged, by tape on the floor or by a large piece of carpet on which the home items are set out. Again, children can be learning that the materials for any one activity area need to stay in that area. This minimizes loss, but also means that any other child who comes to that area can find what they want. It is a helpful exercise for children to realize that every item has its place. They derive some sense of security by knowing that they can always find something in the same place. The impact of the teaching that can be done through the home area is lessened if the home materials are spread out all over the room.

Equipment

What kinds of materials are desirable for the home area? Let's start with the items we can use even with babies, and add to those as we move up the age groups.

A doll is the most basic item for home play. Even a baby can look at a doll and can sit on a teacher's lap with a doll and rock. Babies can look at themselves in an unbreakable mirror, watch goldfish swimming in a clear plastic container or be given fruits and vegetables to look at and touch. Babies who are sitting up and crawling can use plastic saucepans, cups and dishes, a toy telephone or adult-size hats to put on.

Toddlers can begin to use other items with the doll, such as a small blanket, a simple bed or a plastic bowl and spoon for feeding. They may also enjoy playing with handbags. Two-year-olds might enjoy washing a few plastic dishes, empty food boxes and containers and simple food preparation (and tasting!) such as spreading butter on bread or mixing a few fruits to make a salad.

Three-year-olds will enjoy pretending to cook with various plastic dishes, pans and utensils. They will use a child-size cooker or sink if one is available. Bathing the doll is popular, and they can begin to manage simple clothes for the doll. Child-size mops and brooms, dusting cloths and spray bottles with a small amount of water allow for 'cleaning' the room.

Four-year-olds will use a great variety of additional materials. These may include different items of clothing for dressing up, a cash till, an old camera, a doctor or nurse's uniform with wrap-around bandages and a greater number of utensils for pretend cooking. They will also enjoy real food preparation, and a number of suggested activities are listed on p. 155.

Three- and four-year-olds also enjoy various listening activities. Place a portable cassette recorder in the home area and record their conversation for a minute. Play it back to them so they can hear their own voices. Make a recording of various household sounds and see if the children can recognize them – a doorbell ringing, the hoover, the telephone, the toilet flushing, a tap running, etc.

Of course, not all of the items mentioned here would be used every week. They would be added at different times depending on the theme for the session or to create new interest. Additional activities which relate to a theme might be: providing large pieces of fabric for children to dress up as those in Bible times might have dressed; bringing a small suitcase and clothing items for children to pretend to pack for a journey (as for Mary and Joseph's trip to Bethlehem, one of Paul's journeys, or Samuel's trip to the temple at Shiloh to be Eli's helper); having simple woodworking items available, such as blocks of wood, sandpaper, hammer and nails (to be used only with careful teacher supervision!) to help the children learn about the repairing of the temple (King Josiah) or the rebuilding of the walls (Nehemiah).

Any items used in the home area for a particular focus should be removed when that focus is finished. The home area materials should be checked regularly to ensure that they are not broken or cracked and are still safe and suitable for use. Regular sorting also helps prevent the build-up of clutter and unnecessary items. Too many dishes, dolls, clothes, etc. can make the home area look untidy and this is not inviting for children. They may become frustrated when there are too many materials and not actually enough space for using them properly.

This extensive list of home area materials could cost a small fortune to collect. This need not be the case, however. Some basic items will need to be purchased, but many can be made from inexpensive, or even free, materials.

When looking for suitable dolls, keep in mind that the simpler they are, the longer they will last. For home play, dolls that cry, laugh, wet or talk are not necessary. A basic doll that has no 'functions' is best as this is more likely to encourage imaginative play. These kinds of dolls are hard to find these days! You may be able to find one in a jumble or car boot sale – always keep your eyes open for such items. Some suppliers of equipment for play groups may be able to help you. Otherwise, just find the most basic model you can and use that. Soft dolls are better for babies, but plastic dolls are more durable for use by toddlers and older under fives. For under twos, doll clothes are not necessary, and can be frustrating. A child may try to remove them, but be unable to finish the task. Dolls with hair can be unsafe for this age, as well as tending to get very dirty. Three- and four-year-olds may enjoy washing a doll with hair, but under twos do not even notice whether or not the doll has hair.

You may find it necessary to buy plastic dishes and saucepans if no one in your church has a set their children no longer need. Make sure you buy a strong, durable set – they will take harder wear than the average set used by children in the home. Like most things, it is probably better to spend a little more money for a good set that will last longer. If possible, plain dishes without theme motifs (such as My Little Pony or Spot) are better as they are more realistic. If the limited money you have is needed more for other things, you can improvise with the numerous plastic containers left from food used in your home. Margarine containers can be bowls, plastic lids can be plates, larger round containers can become saucepans and even plastic yoghurt pots can be covered with coloured sticky-backed plastic to make cups. A set of strong plastic cutlery would be the only item left to purchase. As these often come in packs of 12, only put out four at a time and replace them as necessary.

Furniture for the home area can be made very inexpensively with a bit of time and creativity. For the youngest children, an empty washing up bowl or a box with a blanket in it makes a doll bed. For twos and above, a strong cardboard box can be adapted to make a doll bed, or a small wooden crate can be sanded smooth and varnished. Likewise, boxes or crates can be turned into cupboards for storing dishes, or cookers. They need not be elaborate. In fact, the simpler they are, the more the children will use their imaginations. Children are very accepting of 'home-made' items in the home corner. Despite the sophisticated toys that are often available, most children play just as happily, and sometimes more creatively, with the basics.

The home area is an important and popular part of any room with under fives. It provides many opportunities for the development of the imagination, social interaction, role play, and meaningful conversation between child and teacher. It can function well even with only a few basic materials that can be added to as time and money allows. Home play experiences can be made available even to babies, and used weekly with all ages under five.

Recipes for the home corner

Orange slush

1 can frozen orange juice (defrosted)
ice cubes

Let the children pour the juice into a liquidizer. Turn it on and let the children feed the ice cubes through the hole in the lid until the mixture is slushy but drinkable. Pour a small amount into cups for each child to taste.

No bake oatmeal cookies

¾ cup sugar
75 grams soft margarine
2 cups uncooked oats
icing sugar

3 Tbs. cocoa
1 Tbs. water
½ tsp. vanilla essence

(N.B.: a cup measure refers to a good size coffee cup or a *small* mug.)
Mix all ingredients except icing sugar. Let the children roll a small spoonful of the mixture into a ball, then roll it in the icing sugar.

Make sure you have warm soapy water available for messy hands!

Honey fruit cups

¼ cup orange juice
1 Tbs. honey

1 apple, 1 orange, 1 banana
1 cup grapes or berries

Mix the orange juice and the honey in a cup. Slice the apple into bite size pieces in a bowl. Pour the orange juice and honey over the apple and mix gently. Cut the rest of the fruit into bite size pieces and add to the apples. Mix gently and spoon into cups for children to taste.
(Washing the cups and spoons afterwards could also be

part of the activity if you are able to provide a washing-up bowl with warm water.)

Orange balls

approx. 6 ounces digestive biscuits
¼ cup orange juice
4 tsp. honey
sugar or icing sugar

Put the biscuits in a plastic bag and let the children help crush them with a rolling pin. Empty the crumbs into a mixing bowl. Add the orange juice and mix with a fork until it looks like wet sand. Add the honey and mix until it all begins to stick together. Give each child a small amount of the mixture to roll into a ball. They can then roll it in the sugar. You can either let the children eat them straight away, or you may want to make a plateful for sharing at group time.

Chocolate rice krispies treats

These are a possibility if you have access to very hot water in order to melt the chocolate. You could bring boiling water in a flask. Of course, extreme care and caution must be taken if you are going to do this. It may be best for the teacher to stir the chocolate while it melts. Then the children can add the krispies and stir. These treats may best be taken home to eat later – we don't want parents wondering why the children won't eat their lunch!

Instant whip

Children will enjoy having a turn with a hand-held rotary beater to make the instant whip. If you have a large group of children, you may need to make up two packets. I would recommend using sugar-free instant whip, made with skimmed or semi-skimmed milk.

Again, you could make washing the cups and spoons part of the activity as well.

Butter

Tip a container of whipping cream into a glass jar with a secure lid. You may want to add a pinch of salt. Let the children take turns shaking it. A teacher with a strong arm will also need to have several turns! The children can watch as the cream turns to butter. When most of the cream has solidified, pour off any excess liquid, and let the children spread the 'butter' on a cream cracker.

This is great fun, but it does require a strong arm!

Peanut butter

Put peanuts in a liquidizer and turn it on. Slowly add oil until it reaches spreading consistency. Let the children spread a little on a cracker or some bread to taste.

This really does work, although the peanut butter may be fairly runny.

Cinnamon toast

Take along an electric toaster. Toast slices of bread, then let children spread margarine on them while still warm. Let them sprinkle on a mixture of cinnamon and sugar. This is usually very popular! (with teachers, too!)

None of these recipes would impress a gourmet chef, but the benefit is in the doing! Many children are not allowed to help with food preparation in the home, so they love having a chance to add ingredients or stir.

To avoid disasters, it might be worth trying out any new recipe at home first. If you don't fancy eating it yourself, you can always find neighbourhood children happy to oblige you!

Remember that any kind of tasting activity can be a good teaching opportunity – it doesn't have to involve a recipe.

Children can taste fruits, raw vegetables (carrots, broccoli, cauliflower and cabbage). In the autumn you may even want to cut open a pumpkin to see what is inside. You can take the seeds home and roast them, then let the children taste them the next week.

Spreading butter or jam on half a slice of bread or on crackers is enjoyable. Again, not all children under five have the opportunity to 'spread their own' at home.

Whenever you use a tasting activity (I would recommend not more than once a month, lest they think they need something to eat every week!) remember that it is just that – *tasting*, not major eating. Some children will want to eat and eat. You will have to limit them so as not spoil their appetites.

Happy cooking!!

Chapter 15

Nature

O Lord, our Lord,
  how majestic is your name in all the earth!

You have set your glory
  above the heavens.
From the lips of children and infants
  you have ordained praise . . .
                              (Psalm 8:1–2)

The heavens declare the glory of God;
  the skies proclaim the work of his hands.
                              (Psalm 19:1)

It is in the wonder and beauty of creation that we see the greatness of God most vividly and clearly portrayed. When we stop to consider the colour, texture and infinite variety of nature, the response of our hearts is worship. We stand in awe of the one who made the universe, the almighty, holy God.

Nature provides us with a superb opportunity to teach young children. They, as we, are fascinated by the miracle of creation. As we explore the natural world with them we can help them understand that God is its maker. As they marvel at its beauty, we can teach them to thank God for what he has made.

There are many different ways we can help even the youngest of babies to begin to appreciate nature. Here are some ideas you may want to use, starting with babies and moving up through the ages.

Flowers and leaves

Provide brightly coloured flowers, a pine cone or some interesting leaves for children to look at. For babies, you may want to put them inside a clear plastic bag that you can seal with tape, or a clear plastic jar. You may hold them on your lap and show them a flower. If they are laying on the floor, you may place it where they can focus on it. As they begin to reach for things, they can touch a plastic jar without damaging the item inside it. As they look at the pine cone in a jar you can say, 'God made the pine cone. Thank you, God, for the pine cone'. As children get older you can provide items for them to look at, smell and touch. If you do not have a low table to put them on, you can use a large tray on the floor. Place a sheet of construction paper on the tray to provide a blank background for the items.

Water play

Let the children enjoy water play. Even a young baby can sit on your lap in front of a shallow pan of water and enjoy splashing his hands (or even his toes in warmer weather!). You may also want to partially fill a small plastic jar with water to which you have added a few drops of blue or green food colouring. As a baby pushes it across the floor, they will enjoy watching it slosh around. Babies who can sit up and hold things will shake it around to watch the water move. As they enjoy watching or splashing in the water, you might say, 'The cool water feels good on your hands (or feet!). Thank you, God, for giving us water'.

Toddlers can wear a plastic apron over their clothes and enjoy splashing their hands in a pan of water. One or two plastic containers added to the water enables them to fill and pour. The floor must be covered, of course, and even with close supervision they may get a bit wet. But, after all, it is only water, and it will dry.

As the children get older they also enjoy sieves and funnels that the water will run through. A variety of objects that float or sink create great interest among four-year-olds. You may also want to provide several clear plastic cups of water. Add red food colouring to one, blue to another and yellow to a third. Then mix the colours and see what other colours you can make. Thank God for all the beautiful colours he has made. Talk about the different things we use water for. Help the children to understand how important water is to us. (If your group of children are very mature you may want to mention that some people do not have enough water to drink, wash, etc. Most under fives, however, find this concept difficult to grasp. Perhaps the best foundation for later understanding is an appreciation for the gift of water that God has given us.)

Pets

Let the children observe a fish. If you do not wish to purchase a small fish, ask someone you know who has fish to bring just one or two in a clear plastic jar of water. You can leave the lid on for the brief time you are using it without hurting the fish. Place it where a baby can see it. For older babies, put it on the floor, but do not allow them to push it around. Toddlers and older children may want to give the fish some food. The children might enjoy singing about the goldfish:

> The goldfish swims in the water,
> The goldfish swims in the water,
> The goldfish swims in the water,
> He likes to swim around.
> > (To the tune of 'The bear
> > went over the mountain'.)

You could substitute the words 'Thank you, God, for the goldfish' in the first three lines.

Other small animals are of great interest to young children. Perhaps someone would bring their bird in its cage, a hamster, or even a rabbit. Make sure none of the children have allergies to any of these. The simplest way of doing this is to put a big sign on the door, saying something like this:

> *Mr. Wilson is bringing his rabbit for us to look at this morning. If your child is allergic to rabbit fur, please will you let us know.*
> > *Thank you*

If you know of someone with small kittens or puppies, a guinea pig or baby chicks, these are all very much enjoyed, too. The size of your classroom and the number of children and teachers you have will determine whether the animal is only brought out for a little while, or if it stays the whole time of the session.

Nature walks

These are always fun for children. This is an activity which is limited to warm, dry weather, so it can't be used often! Nevertheless, it is a very effective way of teaching, and can be repeated several times during a good summer without the children tiring of it. If your church is in a city centre, this may not be feasible for you. Take a short walk around your church by yourself some time and find out what there is to see and hear. You may be surprised. Remember, too, that although a few stray flowers and grass filled with daisies may not be very exciting to you, young children have not seen it as many times as you have. Imagine what it would be like for you to be dropped in the middle of a foreign land. Your eyes would be everywhere at once, taking in all that you have never seen before. This is what nature walks are like for children. I know that my own children even enjoy looking at stones on the path. They may all appear the same to you, but take a closer look – God has made each one different!

You can take a baby in a buggy outside and talk to her about the blue sky or the sound of the birds singing. You may say, 'Thank you, God, for the warm sunshine and the nice breeze'. This can be an effective way of settling a fretful child sometimes. You may want to make sure the parents are happy for their children to go outside. Again, a note on the door is the easiest way to let them all know what you have in mind.

Toddlers will enjoy walking outside, although you may have to enlist one or two extra adults for this activity. Two-, three- and four-year-olds can take a walk with a theme – a listening walk, a colours walk or a leaves walk. One suggestion I have heard for keeping a number of children together is to take a long length of rope and tie knots in it about 18 inches apart. Each child holds on to a knot while walking along!

Older under fives might enjoy being given a paper bag in which to collect twigs, leaves, etc. You could let them decorate the outside of it with crayons beforehand. Write their name on it. They can then take home what they have collected. An alternative to this is to put masking tape loosely around their wrists, sticky side out. They can then stick small leaves, bits of grass or fallen flower petals to it as they walk along.

Nature walks provide many opportunities for songs and conversation about what you see. You can encourage the children to marvel at and appreciate the wonders of God's world firsthand on a walk.

Nature items

Any number of nature items can be brought in for the children to observe. If you are holidaying at the seaside, try to collect as many shells as you can. Children are fascinated by shells. I am very fortunate to have a basket full of shells that my mother collected on the beaches of Florida. I am not sure who is more entranced with them, the children or the adults! No two are exactly alike and the patterns of colour are amazing. How wonderful it is to share with a child that same sense of awe that the psalmist felt.

Interesting rocks and stones, an empty bird's nest (which you have sprayed with disinfectant!), chips of bark, leaves, and blossom from different kinds of trees are all interesting. A variety of vegetable seeds, with the corresponding vegetable, if possible, helps the children understand the growth process. Raw vegetables and fruits for smelling and tasting are always popular. Again, parents need to know what you are tasting.

Sand

Sand is very pleasurable for small children. If you do not have access to sand, ask a family in the church who has a sand pit if they would bring enough to half fill a washing-up bowl. Great care must be taken if you want to let babies experience sand. If you have enough adults to supervise, though, even babies will enjoy the feel of dry sand running over their fingers. As children get older you can add plastic scoops and containers, sieves and funnels. You may want to put shells in the sand for them to bury and find. If you let the parents know that you are using sand they will not be dismayed when they find it in their children's socks or vests later on! Some children manage to get it everywhere, no matter how careful you try to be! Wet sand is fun, but very messy, so in this context it is probably as well to keep it dry.

Flower arranging

Arranging flowers in a vase is fun for three- and four-year-olds. Bring a variety of flowers and greenery from your garden and an unbreakable vase. If your own garden, like mine, is not known for its great abundance of flowers, perhaps a neighbour or friend will supply you with some. It's amazing what people will give you when they know you want it for teaching under fives! You can make a plastic vase by cutting the top off an empty washing-up liquid bottle or bleach bottle. Put some stones or sand in the bottom to weight it, and cover the outside with some pretty paper. Allow the children to arrange and re-arrange the flowers as many times as they want to. If they are in a reasonable state afterwards, an elderly person, or someone who is unwell may enjoy receiving the flowers. If they are in a home-made vase, they won't have to worry about returning it.

Insect watching

Observe insects in a jar. You may be able to capture a bee, a butterfly, some ants or some beetles in a clear jar with air holes punched in the lid. Alternatively, you could cover the top of the jar with a piece cut from an old pair of tights. Secure it around the rim with a tight elastic band. This will let air in, but not let the insects out. All ages will enjoy watching the insects. Make sure you provide a twig or a few leaves according to the type of insect. Treat it kindly, and tell the children that you will let it go after the session. If the weather is fine, they may even want to go outside with you to let a butterfly or a ladybird free. They will enjoy watching it fly away.

You may want to provide a magnifying glass with some nature activities. The children can examine leaves, shells and insects in greater detail if they are magnified.

The list of possibilities for teaching through nature is long and varied. The area in which you live and worship will dictate to you some of the activities you can use. The response of the children may encourage you to think of new ideas, too. There are a few points to bear in mind as you teach through nature:

- Provide real, hands-on experiences of nature for the children. Plastic flowers do not help children understand the smell or feel of a real rose. Carved or moulded animals are nice to play with in the brick area, but they don't enable a child to hear the sound of a bird singing, or watch a fish swimming. Even if you can only provide real nature experiences once a month, it is better to do that well, and make it a fun time of learning.

- If you are able to have a nature table every week, make sure that you change the items regularly so that the children do not tire of them or cease to notice them. If they know that there will be something interesting each time, they will go looking for it.

- Answer the children's questions truthfully, but simply. If you do not know the answer, say so. If they seem keen to know, tell them that you will try to find out for them that week. When things happen in nature which are hard to explain, resist the temptation to call it magic. Mixing blue and yellow to make green is not magic, it is the wonderful creativity of a powerful God.

- Let the children sense your own awe and wonder at what you see around you. As you examine stones and rocks together, rather than explaining the geological processes which cause the striations of colour, allow the children to express their delight at all the different patterns and colours. Let them hear you say, 'I'm so glad God made all these beautiful things for us to enjoy'. Suggest that they might like to say a simple thank-you prayer to God. They can pray with their eyes open as they handle the rocks. 'Thank you, God, for all the pretty colours you made. Amen.'

● Allow the children to discover as much as they can for themselves before you intervene. Place the nature items on a low table or on the floor and wait for the children to notice them. Encourage their curiosity with statements of wonder; 'I wonder how the goldfish breathes in the water'. 'Look how the hamster buries himself in his nest. I wonder why he does that.'

All that God has made declares his glory. Let us revel in the natural world which he has created, and teach the children to do the same.

Chapter 16
Music

The Bible is full of examples of the use of music. Moses and Miriam sang to the Lord after he had parted the waters of the Red Sea. The musicians were placed at the front of the army when King Jehoshaphat faced the armies of Ammon and Moab. David used his gift of music to soothe King Saul with the playing of his harp. As Jesus rode into Jerusalem on a donkey the crowds sang their praise to him. We can surely be in no doubt about the importance of music in our worship of God.

Young children love music. I have rarely met a child under five who did not respond positively to singing or musical instruments. Music can be used to teach, to relax, to encourage movement and creativity and for pure pleasure.

If music is good for children, and music is good for us as Christians, then we ought to be hearing lots of it in our classes of under fives! Most people would readily agree, but some might be more reluctant to use their own voices because they feel they cannot sing well. Not being very tuneful may matter when you are working with older children or adults, but it doesn't make any difference with under fives. They love singing, and are accepting of any voice, even if it isn't fit for the opera house!

Some people may hesitate because they do not have access to a musical instrument to accompany their singing. Again, children under five are not bothered. They like instruments, but they are just as happy singing without them.

How can we use music with under fives, and what kinds of music should we use? Let's answer those questions one at a time.

How to use music

We can use music as a separate activity area during the teaching time, but it is also important to integrate music into all the other activities we provide. Sometimes it is good to have a part of the room where we have home-made instruments for the children to play, or a portable cassette player for them to listen to. We might want to invite someone to bring a guitar, or even a wind instrument, and demonstrate its use. The person would need to be willing to try to answer questions, and to let the children attempt to blow or strum. You may want to think in terms of providing music as a specific activity once every four to six weeks, depending on what is available to you.

Every week, no matter what the children are involved in, you can use music. You can greet a child with a song. You can sing as a child plays in the home area. As you give a baby a bottle you can sing, 'Yes, Jesus loves me'. Babies and toddlers may be soothed and quieted by soft background music, such as instrumental recordings of gentle worship songs. When it is time to tidy up the room, a song can make that time more fun. As the children come for group time, songs can be used to help them relax and prepare to sit still for a few minutes. Songs might reinforce the story. Using instruments or songs that call for various actions (like clapping or marching) recognizes that children are constantly on the move, and attempts to channel some of that movement.

The answer to the question about how and when to use music is basically 'any way you want and any time you can'! There are few times when music is not welcome.

What kind of music?

The answer to the question concerning what *kind* of music to use with under fives has a slightly more complex answer. Before we look at specific songs, let's look at a few basic criteria for appropriate songs. We must use songs that the children can actually sing. Four areas are important.

Range

Children's voices are very limited, so the song needs not to be very high or very low (this is a relief to most adults!).

For the more musical among you, the range needs to stay within the octave from middle C up.

Tune and rhythm

Children will be able to learn and use simple songs more readily than complicated melodies and syncopated rhythms. If you do not know what a syncopated rhythm is, you are unlikely to be trying to use one, so you do not need to worry!

Words

The words need to be literal, concrete and in the vocabulary of an under five. Because young children cannot understand symbolism or abstractions, songs that talk about 'fishers of men' are not helpful. The children do not learn the concept, and may even be confused by it. Songs that use words such as 'hosannah', 'Saviour' or 'redeemer' will not mean a great deal to them either. They may be able to learn the words, but they have no idea what they are singing.

At this point you may be wondering whether this invalidates many of the songs we use in worship every week. You may want to protest that you know young children who can sing all the words to the songs, and really enjoy them. I am sure that is true. I have heard my son, Samuel, go around singing 'My lips shall praise you, my great redeemer'. He seems to be having a great time. I think this is wonderful. I am deeply committed to young children being a part of family worship. I believe that they take in something of what is going on in terms of atmosphere, even when they do not understand the words that are said or sung. (This applies equally to 'good' atmosphere and 'negative' atmosphere.) I think it is important for them to see the whole family of God together, and to see others worshipping.

When we come to teach the under fives as a separate age group, though, we have the opportunity to use specific activities, stories and words that they can understand and relate to. So the songs we use with them in teaching are different from the ones they hear in worship. Some adults seem to find this a problem, but the children don't seem to notice. The children in our church enjoy hearing lively (or quiet!) singing in the large crowd context of worship time. They have the opportunity to hear a variety of instruments being played. But they equally enjoy the simple songs we sing with them in their teaching time.

Actions

If you took a random survey among adults, asking them what kind of songs are best for children, most would invariably say, 'action songs'. Research indicates, however, that under fives find it difficult to concentrate on two things at once. So do some adults! If they are singing a song with actions, they are likely to be thinking more about the actions and less about the words they are singing. This makes it difficult for them to learn anything from the words of the song. The exception to this is when the words of the song describe an action, like clapping hands or tapping feet. These types of songs are very useful, for instance, in group time. We will look at that in a moment.

A very popular song that has been used for years with young children is 'My God is so big, so strong and so mighty'. Children may enjoy singing this song, but they are unlikely to learn much from it. They will be expending too much energy on trying to get the actions right. Also, most children under five do not know what 'mighty' or 'handiwork' mean. The sentiment of the song concerns God's power and his creation. The idea that God can do things that other people cannot do is one we try to teach under fives. They may begin to grasp it, but not in the abstract words of that song. They can, of course, readily relate to God's creativity in nature, so perhaps we would do better to use songs that thank him for the things he has made.

Many adults who grew up in the church will have sung the song that goes like this:

Only a boy called David,
Only a babbling brook.
Only a boy called David,
Five little stones he took.
One little stone went in the sling
and the sling went round and round . . .

. . . and so on. You probably enjoyed that song, and may well be singing it to yourself even as you read the words! But how many children today know what a sling is? There are one or two other difficulties with this story that may make it unsuitable for use with under fives, but we will come to that later. The point here is that the actions may be fun, but they probably do not help the children learn.

The exception we mentioned is songs that describe actions. While these may not teach specifically biblical concepts, they are part of the general growth and development of the whole child. A song that I find very useful with three- and four-year-olds is sung to the tune of 'The bear went over the mountain':

My fingers are starting to wiggle,
My fingers are starting to wiggle,
My fingers are starting to wiggle,
They're wiggling all around.

This is sung several times, moving through the parts of the body – my arms, my legs, my head – and finishes with, 'Now all of me is a-wiggling'. It is difficult to say exactly what spiritual truth this song conveys! But it helps the children in their growing understanding of their bodies, and it recognizes that they need to expend energy constructively before they can be expected to sit and listen to a story.

If all this analysis of words and actions is new to you, you may find it helpful to re-read these last few paragraphs and think through them for a few minutes. Remember that we are not saying any of these songs are wrong or bad for

171

children. We are simply trying to determine what kinds of songs will best help us teach biblical foundations.

So where do we find appropriate songs? You may be able to find a few by listening to children's praise tapes, but most of these are aimed at school age children, so they involve more vocabulary, and begin to deal with concepts and symbolic language.

You will find at the end of this chapter (pp. 174–5) and also in Group Time (pp. 208–9), several songs which I have found to be very useful over the years. They may sound overly simple to you, but children can learn them quickly, and always enjoy singing them.

The other alternative is to make up your own songs. You can use simple, well-known tunes, or you can make up your own melodies. In the section on teaching through activities, you will have found a few examples of simple songs to sing. You will need to practise at home. At first you will probably feel very foolish. But do not judge the songs by adult standards. The songs are not for the grown-ups, they are for the children.

Choose simple words that talk about the theme for the session, or describe one of the activities you are providing. When children are painting at the easel, I often use the words;

> I like to paint,
> I like to paint,
> I like to paint with brushes.

You might also substitute the words, 'It's fun to paint'. I have my own little tune for this song. Why not see if you can make one up?

At clean-up time I use the tune 'Here we go round the mulberry bush' and vary the words to fit the situation. To start the children off, I may sing;

> It's time to put the toys away,
> the toys away, the toys away,
> It's time to put the toys away
> and you can be a helper.

I may then go on to sing, 'Joshua can put the bricks away
. . . and he can be a helper', or any other child's name and
the job I would like them to do. As well as making it more
fun, it helps the children know exactly what to do. If you
just say, 'It's time to tidy up now', most children won't
know where to start. But if you give them a specific task
to do, they will respond.

Suppose the story you are using is Ruth, Boaz and
Grandmother Naomi, and the aim is to help the children
understand that families love us and look after us. As a
child rocks or baths the doll in the home corner, you could
make up a tune for words like this:

> Naomi rocked her grandson, she loved
>   him very much.
> Thank you, God, for Grandma, she loves
>   me very much.

Or, to a different tune:

> Ruth looked after her baby, Mummy
>   looks after me.
> Boaz looked after his baby, Daddy
>   looks after me.

You may make up one or two songs for a particular session
and only use them that day. Sing them to the children,
but do not worry if they do not sing them with you. Other
songs with more general themes you may use again and
again. These songs are best learned by repetition, rather
than sitting the children down and trying to teach them
line by line. The more you 'write' your own songs, the
easier you will find it. If you feel very non-musical, and
can't seem to get started, show these pages to a friend who
can sing, and ask for help.

It has been said that music is a universal language. It
certainly seems to cross many barriers. Use it freely and
frequently with the children. They will enjoy it and so will
you. Not only will it bring pleasure and reinforce learning,

Sharing Jesus with under fives

it can also ease a fretful child and provide a happy, relaxed atmosphere.

> Come, let us sing for joy to the LORD . . .
> Let us come before him with thanksgiving
>   and extol him with music and song.
>
> (Psalm 95:1–2)

> It is good to praise the LORD
>   and make music to your name, O
>   Most High.
>
> (Psalm 92:1)

What better incentive could we have for using joyful music than the commands of Scripture!

Songs for under fives

Stories from the Bible

Sto-ries from the Bi-ble. Sto-ries from the Bi-ble. I like to hear my tea cher* tell sto-ries from the Bi-ble.

* substitute mummy or daddy (Stories about Jesus, David, Samuel, etc.)

Jesus loves me

Je - sus loves me.　Je - sus loves me.

I love Je - sus.　I love him.

I can help

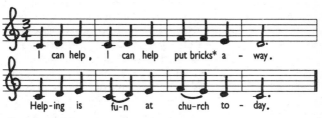

I can help, I can help put bricks* a - way.

Help-ing is fu-n at chu-rch to - day.

*toys, books, paint

Chapter 17

Using the Bible

We have looked at many ways to communicate biblical principles through the use of various activities and hopefully, you will have received several new ideas about how to teach the Bible to under fives in a meaningful way. In this section we will talk about how to use the Bible specifically, so that children not only hear about it, but they also see it and touch it. This is the first step towards learning to love God's word, and to read it and study it for themselves.

The relevance of the Bible to under fives

Over the years that I have worked with under fives, I have seen that they are fascinated by the Bible. I have a little girl in my class at the moment who loves to look at the Bible. Because of the young age of my class, I leave the Bible on a table out of reach, unless I am able to supervise it. I want the children to use it, but I don't want them to abuse it. Many times, though, when I have been involved with other children, I look up to find that Marie has managed to pull the Bible off the table, and is sitting looking at the pictures. At the end of the session, when we are all sitting down together, the children may be restless. But as soon as I put the Bible on my lap, and start to tell them a story, or sing about what the Bible says, they are spellbound.

Older under fives like to know what the Bible says. And they always seem to be able to remember it for someone else! Many is the time I have been told quite piously by a four-year-old, 'The Bible says "Be kind". Jonathan isn't being kind to me'. My own children manage to remember what the Bible says when it is to their advantage. Once I was eating some sweets when one of them came and asked for some. When I said no, I was promptly reminded, 'But you have to give me some, because the Bible says that we should share!'

At times they quote the Bible inappropriately, but other times they get it spot on. When they see someone shouting at or hitting another person in public, or they see violence on the news, they know that isn't what the Bible says. 'Mummy, why are they doing that? The Bible says to be kind, and that isn't kind, is it?' Don't let anyone tell you that children under five can't begin to know and apply God's word!

In many ways, the Bible is a difficult book, and we struggle to understand it, even as adults. It is probably the more difficult portions of the Scriptures that people have in mind when they ask, 'What can you teach children under five?'

Think about all the parts of the Bible that we *do* understand. There are some passages which leave us in no doubt about their meaning and application. Many of these can be passed on even to very young children in ways they can understand. Ephesians 4:32, which was mentioned above, says, 'Be kind . . . to one another'. I don't know about you, but I don't need a commentary to tell me what that means!

Large chunks of the Bible are also very clear in their message. Although we may not read the Genesis account of creation word for word to a two-year-old, the undeniable message is, 'God made the world'. Whatever you may believe about how he did it, and how long it took him, the basic truth is that the beauty around us has its origins in the creator God. This is well worth teaching to our children!

Many of the stories in the Bible, both Old and New Testament, show us how God wants us to live. Others help us understand his love for us, or tell us about Jesus. Using these stories with under fives helps them to relate biblical principles to actual happenings. The next step from there is translating that into everyday living.

Despite some of the difficulties we encounter in trying to understand and apply God's word to our lives, there is much that we understand very well. This is what we want to pass on to our children in their early years. We do not need to bother them with the things we struggle over. With great joy, we want to give them a foundation in the certainties of our faith.

Introducing the Bible

Where, then, do we start? How do we use the Bible with very young children? It might be most helpful if we start with babies and progress from there. This will help give a framework, based on the development of the child physically, mentally and spiritually.

Parents and others are keen to talk to babies from the moment they are born. We tell them that we love them, that they are beautiful, or we talk to them about who we are and what we are doing. In other words, it is natural for us to tell them those things which we feel are important even before they begin to understand. This is the way they should learn about the Bible – naturally, and from the beginning.

A newborn baby hears you when you say, 'I love you. The Bible says that Jesus loves you, too'. As you greet a baby in your room at church, he can hear you say, 'Good morning, Thomas. I'm glad you came to church today. The Bible tells us that Jesus went to church with his family. You have come to church, too.' No one knows at what point Thomas begins to understand those words, so we use them from his earliest days.

As you read these examples of things we can say to even the youngest of babies, you may dismiss them as simplistic. They are simple, not simplistic. They are, in fact, very profound. The problem is, we imagine them being said in that phony, sickly sweet voice that so many adults use when talking to babies. As we talk to children about the truths of God's word, we must use a warm, natural voice. There is no need for a put-on tone that implies insincerity.

As we meet the physical needs of babies, we can relate that to the Bible. If you are giving a baby a bottle, you can say, 'You are enjoying your milk, Jodi. The Bible says that God gives us things to enjoy. Thank you, God, for Jodi's milk' (I Tim. 6:17). As Jodi learns to focus her eyes, you can sit with her in your lap and hold the Bible open. As she looks at it, you might sing, 'The Bible is a special book, it tells us Jesus loves us'. (This is another chance to make up your own tune!) You might also open it to I Samuel and say, 'The Bible tells us about a boy called Samuel. His mother took him to the big church at Shiloh so that he could help teacher Eli. Samuel was a helper at church'. For a young baby, these kinds of things are a good introduction to the Bible. They help them to understand that the Bible is about familiar things. This relates the Bible to everyday life rather than consigning it to irrelevance.

As babies reach the age when they are sitting up by themselves, you may want to sit next to them, and show them pictures in the Bible. If you do not have a Bible with suitable pictures, you can use your own Bible. Provide a picture to illustrate what you are talking about. For example, you may have some pictures of birds. You can place these next to the Bible. As a baby looks at the pictures, you can say, 'These are birds. The Bible says that God made the birds. Look at all the different kinds of birds God made'. If you are looking at a picture book of animals, you may be naming the various ones and imitating their sounds. As you come to a picture of a sheep, you could say, 'In the Bible we read about David. He helped his father by looking after the sheep. He found them green grass to eat, and water to drink'. Again, this reinforces the truth that the Bible has to do with our lives every day.

It is good for babies to hear about people in the Bible. A few sentences that convey a particular theme are sufficient. When they are older they will hear and remember whole stories about biblical characters. In the beginning it is enough that they hear about real people doing real things that they can relate to.

Somewhere around eighteen months to two years children start to listen to and take in very short stories. When this happens we can begin to use brief, simple stories from the Bible. We can tell them a few sentences of a story as they are involved in different activities. If there is some form of group time, they can hear the story again then.

Toddlers need not only to hear Bible stories, but also Bible verses and thoughts that relate to what they are doing. Some Bible verses are simple enough in their vocabulary and structure that we can use them as direct quotes. Ephesians 4:32, mentioned above, is one example. Another might be Proverbs 17:17, 'A friend loves at all times.' We can use the verse exactly as it stands to help children understand about being kind or being friends. Other, factual verses give children helpful information. Matthew 2:1 says, 'Jesus was born in Bethlehem.' Matthew 19:14 says, 'Jesus said, ''Let the little children come to me'' '.

Other verses in the Bible communicate important truths, but the words or phrases are beyond the understanding of a child under five. We can paraphrase those verses into language that is on their level. One of the best examples of this is Psalm 122:1. The NIV translation says, 'I rejoiced with those who said to me, ''Let us go to the house of the LORD'' '. If you say that to a three-year-old they will want to know two things. Firstly, what does 'rejoice' mean? Secondly, does the Lord's house have an upstairs like mine and are we staying there for tea?

A three-year-old might better understand the real meaning of this verse if they hear, 'I was glad when they said, ''Let's go to church'' '. For a younger child an even simpler way to communicate the essence of this verse might be, 'I like to go to church'.

Many adults are impressed when young children memorize Bible verses. They think that the children are 'learning the Bible'. Perhaps it is more accurate to say they are learning to quote the Bible. I think we would be true to the message of the Scriptures if we say that God is more concerned that we understand and obey the spirit of the Bible than be able to quote the letter of the Bible without true understanding.

Most adults would gladly agree that we need to tell children Bible stories in language they can understand. They would not advocate reading the stories directly from the text to a two-year-old. Rephrasing Bible verses, without changing their intended meaning, is exactly the same principle. The most important thing is to help our children grow up to see that the Bible is alive, and makes a difference to their lives now. I would rather see my own children demonstrate the characteristics described in the Beatitudes (Matthew 5) than be able to quote them from memory. (Of course, when they are old enough to understand the words, it would be nice for them to live them and memorize them!)

Hopefully this rather lengthy explanation will help you understand why, in this section on 'Using the Bible', many of the examples cited do not directly quote the Scriptures. The words may not be those you find in the NIV or even the Good News Bible, but they convey the meaning intended. Some other examples of paraphrasing Bible verses are given at the end of this section.

As children reach three or four years of age, they can understand and listen to greater detail in Bible stories. During activity time it may be appropriate only to tell a small portion of the story for that day. At group time they can hear the whole story. They will listen and understand more if they have heard one or two sentences from the story during the session.

Three- and four-year-olds can also understand more Bible verses and thoughts. They may be able to repeat them after you have said them. It is good to encourage this, but not in any way that implies that a child who can say a verse is better or more clever than one who can't. Children will be helped to know and love the Bible when it is used in positive ways, rather than in 'competitive' ways.

It is good to have the Bible as available as possible to children during the session. If you are working with babies or toddlers, they can only use it with supervision, so it cannot be left lying on the floor. With children above toddler age you may want to place the Bible in one of the activity areas each week. Open it to an appropriate verse, and lay a marker made of coloured construction paper on the page. On the marker write the reference and the verse, either as it is, or paraphrased, if that is more appropriate.

Bible activities

Sometimes, you may want to use the Bible as an activity in itself. I find that most children are very interested to know what the Bible says. Here are a few suggestions you may find helpful:

Make several markers out of different colours of paper

On each one write a reference and the verse or paraphrase. Put them in the correct places in the Bible, with about two inches of the marker sticking out at the top. As a teacher sits with the Bible, children will wander over to see what she is doing. Let a child choose a marker, then open the Bible and say, 'The Bible says . . .' For a two-year-old, this may be enough. A three- or four-year-old may want to repeat the verse, either with the teacher, or alone. Some children may want to talk about the verse. Let the children take turns choosing markers. It doesn't matter if several children choose the same one. If this keeps happening, though, you may want to slide a marker right down inside the Bible after it has been chosen. Let the next child choose a different one, and so on, until all the markers have been chosen. You can then slide them all up again and start over. Let this go on as long as children are interested. Some may come and go after only one verse, others may stay for 10 or 15 minutes. When interest seems to wane, the teacher can put the Bible away, and involve herself in another activity area.

Play a matching game with markers

For each marker you make for the Bible, make another blank one the same colour. Let a child choose a blank marker, then find the matching colour in the Bible. This can be managed by some older two-year-olds. They may not be able to say their colours, but they can match by sight. For three- and four-year-olds, you may want to make the matching of a different type. You might make all the markers the same colour, but at the top of each one put a sticker. Each one could have a different shape or colour. Make two of each so that the children can match them up. You may be able to find matching pictures, such as flowers, by obtaining two identical gardening catalogues.

Throw a bean bag to choose a marker

For each coloured marker you make, cut a circle of the same colour. The circle should be three to five inches in diameter. Spread the circles out on the floor and let the children take turns gently throwing a beanbag. Whichever circle it lands on (or nearest to!) is the colour they must find in the Bible. Again, if the same colour keeps coming up, you may want to remove a circle once it has been landed on, until all circles are gone.

These 'games' stimulate interest, and help the children really enjoy seeing what the Bible says. They encourage participation, even amongst the more shy children, because there are no winners or losers. A child can play without any fear of failing.

Choosing Bible stories

Taking into consideration all that we have said about how children learn and understand things, what would be the aims and/or criteria for a Bible story for under fives?

- It must be fairly simple.
- It would involve events that under fives know about or can relate to.
- It would illustrate a biblical principle that they can understand.
- It would be concrete, about real people and specific happenings.

What are some stories that would or would not fit in this framework?

The story of creation can be told simply. It may be best broken up into three or four stories over as many weeks. The story of creation involves things children know about – sun, moon, plants, rivers, animals and people. It helps them to understand that 'God made the world'. Although we do not know how God made the world, we emphasize all the things he did make. I have rarely been asked how God made these things. (Not by a child, anyway!) If a child did ask, this story illustrates another important truth. You could say, 'That's a good question. I don't know exactly how God made the animals. But the Bible tells us that God can do things people cannot do. You and I cannot make an animal, but God can, and he did'.

The story of Ruth staying with Naomi and finding grain to make bread teaches something important: families love and look after one another. This story has real people in it, can be told simply, and is about something children know about – needing food to eat, and taking care of people we love.

What about the story of David and Goliath? This is certainly an exciting story, and it could be told simply. Beyond that, however, it does not fit the aims. It is about things that children do not understand – a giant, slingshots, armies and killing. Although the story is real and concrete, its significance is symbolic: no matter how small and unimportant you may feel, God can use you. This is a wonderful truth, but it is beyond the understanding of young children. There are details in this story which may be frightening or confusing to an under five. Giants are not generally portrayed in fairy stories as friendly. Although those giants are not real, this one was. We cannot say that it is just a story. Why would it be all right for David to kill someone? Killing doesn't make people happy. Why would God want David to do that? These questions are hard enough to answer when we can think symbolically, and understand conceptually. Rather than raise them with under fives, perhaps it is better to leave this story until they can better grasp its significance.

The same difficulties would arise with some of the other 'popular' stories in the Old Testament, such as Jonah, Daniel in the Lions' Den, and Joshua and the Walls of Jericho. These stories may be suitable for teaching older children, but they may not be the best for teaching under fives.

In the New Testament, there are many stories about Jesus that help young children understand how he loved people, that he did good things and that he told us how God wants us to live. In case you are thinking that this sounds like a fairly weak approach to who Jesus is, remember that under fives cannot understand about God as Father, about Jesus taking our place on the cross, or about the revolutionary nature of what Jesus said and did. They can understand that Jesus made sick people well; that he taught us that God loves and takes care of the birds, and he loves and takes care of us; that Jesus had friends (Mary and Martha are two we know something about); and that Jesus went to church.

The parables of Jesus are symbolic in their meaning and are therefore difficult for under fives to benefit from. The wise and foolish builders is a great story, but young children have no idea what foundations are – in life or in buildings!

The parable of the talents, the sheep and the goats, and the lost coin are all interesting, and teach us important things. Although it may be possible to explain the symbolism of these stories in words that the children can understand – and I know people who say this is the case – I would have doubts about whether they could meaningfully make the connection between a lost coin being found, and God's joy at people becoming Christians. There are many Bible stories that clearly illustrate what we would be wanting to teach under fives. Why use symbolic parables that we have to adapt in order for them to understand?

The parable that is an exception is the story of the Kind Man (known to us as the Good Samaritan). It illustrates being kind to others. The more subtle issues in the story, like racism and stuffy religiosity, are better left for a later age. You can use the main facts, though, and begin it by saying, 'One time Jesus told the people who were listening to him a story about a man who . . .'

New Testament stories about Paul, Aquila and Priscilla, Lydia, Philip, and others all illustrate different biblical principles. Each of these people loved Jesus and told others about him. The story of Paul's conversion may perhaps be too difficult, but there are many stories of him working with others, going to different places telling about Jesus, and writing letters to his friend (Timothy, in particular) that under fives can learn from.

When choosing Bible stories and teaching aims for under fives, remember that it is not necessarily the most well-known stories that are the best. Stories such as King Josiah repairing the church, and David and his friend Jonathan can effectively teach under fives important foundational truths.

Much of our Christian teaching today focuses on the New Testament, and the more familiar stories and characters in the Old Testament. Using some of the more 'obscure' stories as well can give under fives a good foundation for later understanding how God deals with his people. When we read the passages in order to condense the stories, we may find that God teaches *us* some things, or helps us to see them in a new way.

In the following section, you will find some suggested stories for under fives. As you become familiar with how they are used to teach spiritual truth, you will be able to choose and condense other Bible stories yourself.

The Bible is a very special book. It is a history book, a poetry book, a hymn book and an exciting narrative. It is the only book that claims to be living and active. It is a relevant guide for all our lives. It helps us understand the God who made us, loves us and is faithful to us. The Bible reveals Jesus, our Saviour and our Lord. May God help us to teach our children to love and respect, and, most importantly, to live out this most holy word.

Paraphrases for use with under fives

Verse	Paraphrase
Genesis 1:11 'Then God said, "Let the land produce vegetation: seed-bearing plants and trees on the land that bear fruit with seed in it, according to their various kinds." And it was so'.	God made trees. God made fruit. God made grass. God made flowers.
Genesis 1:27 'So God created man in his own image, in the image of God he created him; male and female he created them'.	God made people.
Exodus 20:12 'Honour your father and your mother, so that you may live long in the land the LORD your God is giving you'.	Love your father and mother.
Job 37:14 'Listen to this, Job; stop and consider God's wonders'.	Think of all the wonderful things God made.
Psalm 71:23 'My lips will shout for joy when I sing praise to you—I, whom you have redeemed'.	I will sing happy songs to God.
Psalm 33:1 'Sing joyfully to the LORD, you righteous; it is fitting for the upright to praise him'.	It is good to sing thanks to God.

Luke 2:52 'And Jesus grew in wisdom and stature, and in favour with God and men'.

Jesus grew up. Jesus had friends.

Luke 4:16 'He went to Nazareth, where he had been brought up, and on the Sabbath day he went into the synagogue, as was his custom. And he stood up to read'.

Jesus went to church. Jesus read the Bible at church.

John 15:12 'My command is this: Love each other as I have loved you'.

Jesus said, 'Love each other'. Jesus loves you.

Acts 10:38 'how God anointed Jesus of Nazareth with the Holy Spirit and power, and how he went about doing good and healing all who were under the power of the devil, because God was with him'.

Jesus did good things. Jesus went to many places and did good things. Jesus made sick people well.

2 Corinthians 1:24 'Not that we lord it over your faith, but we work with you for your joy, because it is by faith you stand firm'.

We work together.

Colossians 1:3 'We always thank God, the Father of our Lord Jesus Christ, when we pray for you . . .'

We thank God for you.

I Timothy 6:18 'Command them to do good, to be rich in good deeds, and to be generous and willing to share'.

Be ready to share. It is good to share. God wants us to do good things.

I Peter 5:7 'Cast all your anxiety on him because he cares for you'.

God cares for you.

I John 4:10 'This is love: not that we loved God, but that he loved us and sent his Son as an atoning sacrifice for our sins'.

God loves us. God loved us and sent his Son.

This list is not exhaustive. It only gives an introduction to the way verses can be paraphrased, in addition to the examples cited in earlier paragraphs.

Choosing a Bible for use with under fives

In recent years a variety of Bibles have been published with children in mind. The layout and the pictures reflect this decade rather than the 1950s. I have even seen in the last year a Bible that is intended for use with toddlers. These attempts to make the Bible relevant and accessible to even the youngest of children are to be commended.

With such a wide choice of Bibles on the market, it is important that we choose carefully. Some of the modern Bibles use cartoon-style pictures. Although bright and attractive, they are not very realistic. They may not help us in trying to teach children that the Bible is about real people in real places. Some of the 'Bibles' produced for under fives are not actually Bibles, but are books of Bible stories. These may be very helpful for use in the home, although they, too, often have cartoon-type pictures.

The *New International Children's Bible* was published a few years ago. It is a special translation designed for children ages 6–12 to be able to read and understand for themselves. This Bible would be excellent for use with school age children. The pictures in it are more realistic than some others, but many of them illustrate stories which are not very appropriate for under fives, like Jonah and the big fish. Although I would recommend it for older children, I am not sure that it would be the best for under fives.

Unless another Bible is available now, it may be that you

will not find one that you feel has suitable pictures for use with under fives. You can use your own Bible with the children for marking verses and paraphrases. You may be able to find pictures to illustrate the Bible stories you use. If not, you can use the Bible without pictures. This is preferable to using pictures that do not clarify or reinforce what you are teaching.

If you ever travel to the United States and have access to a Baptist Book Store, you may want to look at the Holman *Read-to-me*[1] edition of the Bible. It comes in different translations, but all contain the same pictures. It also has suggestions for using the Bible with under fives. At the back there are a number of Bible stories written in language suitable for under fives. This is the Bible my own children have, and the one that we use with under fives at church.

---

[1] *Holy Bible – Read to Me Edition* (Holman Bible Publishers, Nashville, 1984).

Chapter 18

Group time

Group time with under fives can be very productive. It has the potential for building relationships, developing social skills and reinforcing and further teaching the Bible theme for the session.

But it can also be disastrous! Working with young children is unpredictable at the best of times. When you get them all sitting together in a group, you never know what might happen next. Sometimes it's the things they do, but more often, it is the things they say.

I have heard many revelations about what has gone on in some of the homes during the week. I've also been on the other end of that when my own children's teachers have come to me and said, 'We heard all about you dropping the milk jug on the floor this morning!'

I remember one time when I was talking with a group of three-year-olds about things we like to do, and having fun. 'What do you like to do?', I asked. With total sincerity one little girl said, 'I like to pick my nose'! The children may have wondered why I suddenly had a choking fit!

Group time is not without its risks. But the potential benefits outweigh these considerably. The best insurance against embarrassing moments is being prepared. As we understand the who, when, where, what and how of group time, we can approach it with greater confidence and enthusiasm.

Who?

Opinions about what age is appropriate for group time may vary. Certainly you would expect to be having such a time with children three and above. I have used some form of group time with two-year-olds, and even with toddlers.

Many factors may influence what age you begin trying

to provide some type of group experience for children. If you have a room with mixed ages, you will have to think carefully about whether you can actually manage group time. If you have more than one teacher, you may be able to use part of the room for group time with the older ones. You may have a group of two-year-olds with very mixed levels of maturity. Some may be able to cope with a group activity, others may not. You may decide to start with only two or three minutes, and slowly increase it to seven or eight minutes.

The length of time you have for your teaching session may also affect how you structure things. If you have an hour, you will not have any trouble fitting in meaningful group time. If you only have 20 to 30 minutes, you may feel that the younger children will benefit more by continuing teaching activities for the whole session.

In the section, 'What?' to do in group time, we will consider ideas for children as young as toddlers. Below that age, one-to-one interaction between babies and teachers is the most effective means of teaching spiritual truth.

When?

The best time for group time is probably at the end of the session. There are a number of reasons for this:

- It allows children time beforehand to expend their energy in productive ways.
- It allows for much good teaching to happen during activity time. This makes children more receptive to the theme or story because they may have already encountered it in the various activities. Of course, there will not always be natural opportunities to share some of the Bible story in every activity area every week. Having group time ensures that each child has a chance to hear the Bible story.
- Group time at the end means that the room can be tidied from activity time – helping to put things away is part of learning, too.
- Having group time when the children have finished their other activities means they are not looking around

at what they want to do after group time. It also means that they can concentrate better because they are not thinking of the artwork they left half-finished, anxiously wondering when they will be able to get back to it.

Group time seems to fit most naturally at the end of the session. If, for various reasons, you must have it some other time, it can still be equally valuable.

Time scheduling

Making the most of teaching time on Sundays is important, whether it is twenty minutes or an hour. Finding the time schedule that works best for you may only come through trial and error. The way you divide your time depends on many factors – the number and ages of children, room size, the number of teachers, and the amount of time you have.

Those who teach the babies and youngest toddlers are the least affected by the length of time. If time is short, it may be appropriate to provide only one new or different activity each week, in addition to the regular things you have. If you have 30 minutes or less, I would recommend teaching through activities only, and not trying to fit in group time with children up to the age of about two and a half. For older toddlers and children over two, you may want to think in terms of having two 'new' activities each week.

If you are teaching children between two and a half and five, and you have half an hour or less, you may want to think of trying 20–25 minutes of activity time followed by a brief group time. Perhaps you could ask the children to do only the minimum of clearing away. Although it is important for them to learn to help with this, if your time is limited, it may be better used in activities and group time. If you find that it is too rushed, you may want to use only activities, and ensure that one activity each week provides an opportunity for using the Bible story with the children who are involved in it. You may want to make the Bible the centre of an activity area, and through the use of pictures or music make that area a place for 'mini' group time.

When time is short the temptation is to keep the children in a group the whole time, possibly only providing an art activity which involves all the children doing the same thing at the same time. Although this may be easier for the teacher, it may not be best for the children. I would still want to see at least two, and probably three, choices of activity where meaningful teaching occurs, followed by a brief group time.

Of course, if you have a longer time, 45 minutes to an hour, you can more easily allow for teaching through activities, time for putting things away, and group time. Because we have an hour for teaching, we can have 40–45 minutes for activities. This may sound like a long time, but with a variety of interesting activities and well prepared teachers, it goes quickly. Occasionally there is a day when it seems to drag, and I think my watch must have stopped, but these are few, and are usually more to do with me than with the children.

However long (or short!) your time may be, you can provide meaningful teaching for under fives. Don't be afraid to experiment with different schedules. Try one for several weeks. If it doesn't seem quite right, try something else. If you continue to provide good teaching even through transition, the children will feel secure. They will not suffer unduly from your attempts to get it right.

Where?

If you have a room with babies up to five year olds, you may find that it is helpful to take the older ones out of the room for group time. Even a quiet hallway might enable them to concentrate more easily. In general, though, the best place to have group time is in the same place you have activity time. If the room is small, it may be necessary to move things to the edges to make enough space.

If you have child-sized chairs, you may want to use them

for children three and above. Chairs are certainly not necessary, though. Because we meet in a school, I have used the floor for group time for nearly eight years. Children don't mind where they sit. It is only teachers whose legs may get a bit stiff on the floor!

If the children are sitting on the floor, it is generally better for the teacher to sit on the floor. I have made an exception to this when I have taught a large class of children. Because there were about twenty of them, I found it was easier for them all to see me if I sat on a low chair, rather than on the floor.

Sitting the children in a circle is usually the best arrangement. If they are in rows, the ones in the back cannot see. Children often need assistance arranging themselves into some kind of circle. A teacher other than the one who is leading group time can help with this, or it can be made into a game. We will look at some ideas for this under the 'What?' of group time.

What and how?

Considering who group time is for, and when and where it should be is like building a skeleton. Looking at what we do and how we do it puts flesh on those bones. Group time may have several components, and these vary in length according to the age of the children. We will look at the different possibilities, then at how we might put them together to make an effective group time.

Movement songs or rhymes

At various points during group time, children need the opportunity to move around. They find it almost impossible to sit still for more than a few minutes. Channelling their energy recognizes their need for movement, and uses it productively. Simple songs which describe movements are appropriate. In the section on music, the 'Wiggle Song' was mentioned (p. 171). Other, similar songs are useful and are always enjoyed by children. Various rhymes that require certain movements are valuable, too. They not only direct energy, but they are part of physical development. At the end of this section there are a number of suggested songs and rhymes.

'Name' songs and games

Children love to hear their own name said or sung. All the children I have ever worked with respond well to a simple song that uses their name. You may go around the circle singing to each child, 'I have a good friend, — is his/her name'. Some of the children will sing with you, others may not. Or you might sing, 'I am happy, I am happy, — is here today'. (These songs can also be used when greeting a child at the beginning of the session, or to any child during activity time.)

For three- and four-year-olds you can play games that involve naming children. You might describe what a child is wearing and see if the children can guess who it is. You might name two children and ask them to swap places. (This is an excellent game for subtly separating 'troublemakers'!) Or you might name one child and ask them to name another child. Then the two change places in the circle. These are good exercises for a teacher's memory, as it is important to make sure that each child's name is used!

Using the Bible

Most of the suggestions given in the section entitled 'Using the Bible' can be used during group time. If you have a large number of children, you may not be able to let them all have a turn at choosing or matching markers. You can explain that there will not be time for everyone to have a turn, but that other children will have a turn next week. This is very difficult for some children to understand or accept, but it, too, is part of the development process. (This is another time for teacher's memory to be sharp – remembering from one week to the next!) If not all children have had a turn to participate in such an activity, you may be able to use it again at the very end, while waiting for children to be collected.

Conversation

Group time is an important time for talking with children as well as to them. Let them tell you about the different things they have been doing during the session. You may want to ask questions about the different activities that were available that day. 'Who painted this morning?' 'Did I see a new puzzle today?' 'I saw some children tasting something this morning. Who would like to tell me about it?'

It is a good idea to remind children to raise their hands if they want to tell you something. This may sound like school, but really, it is just good common sense and courtesy. If several children want to talk, you could say, 'Mark wants to tell us something now. After that it will be Alistair's turn, then Lorena's'. Some children will soon get into the habit of remembering to raise their hand. Other children are always bursting to talk, and they have trouble remembering. A gentle reminder is often necessary. 'Aaron, I know you want to tell me something. It will be your turn in a minute. Stephen has raised his hand, and it is his turn now.'

Many of today's children are hungry for conversation. Some of them do not have an adult who regularly wants to listen to what they have to say. For these children, not only is group time conversation important, but special care can be taken at other times to listen to them.

Conversation can be woven into all the elements of group time. You can talk about activities, about the story, about the theme for the day. Often children have something they want to tell you about – a special outing, a birthday party, or any number of things (like their mum dropping the milk jug!). It takes time to get the balance right between giving the children important opportunities to develop in conversation, and not letting that become the only feature of group time.

Bible stories

I believe it is important for children to hear a story from the Bible each week. You may not use a 'Bible marker game' with them each week, but they need to see the Bible used in group time. As the teacher tells the story, he can hold the Bible open on his lap to the correct reference.

Most children under five will not remember the details of a Bible story. That is okay. When they are older they will have time for remembering. Many years ago I told the story of the Kind Man (The Good Samaritan) to a group of three-year-olds. I later discovered that one little girl went home and told her father that we had a story about a man who fell off a donkey! So much for details! The important thing is not that they can recite the story later at home, but that they hear a story related to a theme they can understand.

For example: if you tell the story of Ruth looking after Naomi, they will probably not remember the names, unless they happen to know a child called Ruth or Naomi. They may not remember that she chose to stay with Naomi, and helped her find grain for bread. The important part is the connection between the story and living out what the Bible says. I would far rather have them remember that God planned for families to take care of one another, and to say thank you to God for their own families, than to remember that collecting grain is called 'gleaning'!

The Bible story is an essential part of group time. It helps children understand that the theme is not just some nice words that are a good idea. They are a good idea because they are from the Bible, they are God's words.

Other games

There are a number of other 'games' you can use at group time. I find it is always a good idea to have one in mind because you never know quite how the time will go. Some weeks children are interested in the Bible story and want to talk about it. Some weeks they all want to tell about something they did. Other times they are relatively quiet, or the things you have planned don't seem to spark their attention. It is always good to have more planned than you have time for. This allows for these fluctuations.

For toddlers and two-year-olds, the 'game' could be as simple as 'Can you?' You ask them to do simple things. Can you clap your hands, stamp your feet, march around the room, wave your arms, etc. Or you may provide a simple activity, such as blowing bubbles for them, or rolling a ball. Make the circle of children larger and roll the ball to each child in turn. You could sing, 'Roll the ball to —, roll it back to me'. Or you might want to give each child a small amount of playdough to squeeze and press.

For three- and four-year-olds, you may want to have a 'feel bag'. In a cloth bag, or an old pillowcase, place several familiar objects. The children take turns putting a hand in the bag and grasping an object. They can feel it in the bag and try to guess what it is without looking. Things like a small hairbrush, a toothbrush, a comb, a brick, a teaspoon, a pencil or crayon, a small ball or a cotton wool ball would all be suitable.

Using the same types of objects, you can play 'what's missing?'. Arrange the objects on a tray and let the children name them all. Ask them to close or cover their eyes while you take an object away. Then ask them to look and raise their hand if they know what is missing.

A variation of this game for older three- and four-year-olds is to place eight to ten objects on a tray. After the children have named them all, cover the items with a cloth. See how many of the objects the children can recall.

Involve the children in using their senses by playing 'I hear, I touch, I see'. Describe an object in the room by saying whether you hear it, touch it or see it, then give clues about it and see if the children can guess what it is.

Singing

In addition to songs that involve using children's names, you will want to use other songs. These may be songs that reflect the theme, or that relate to conversation. If the children have been telling you about all the things they have done that session, you may want to sing,

I like to go to church,
I like to go to church,
I like the happy things we do,
  I like to go to church.

(see p. 174 for tune.)

I am a musician, so using songs spontaneously is easy for me. For those who are less musical, more planning is required. Have a song or two in mind for each part of group time. If it seems appropriate, use it. When the children are talking about something, such as the activities as mentioned above, I often say, 'I know a song about that'. I then sing the song to them and then usually say, 'Let's sing it again. You can sing it with me this time'. Some children will pick up a tune immediately. Others will try to join in. Some children will rarely sing themselves, but they enjoy listening to you sing.

Music is an excellent tool. It helps children understand and remember things they have been learning. It involves even the most shy children, because they can participate by listening. It recaptures their interest and focuses their attention. And, in addition, it is good fun!

Prayer

Most of the prayers prayed by children in the context of group time will be thank you prayers. What a good foundation that is! Many of us as adults would do well to pray more thank you prayers! It is good to allow those children who want to, to pray in group time. Their prayers need some guidance. After telling the Bible story about Jesus helping a blind man to see, you could say, 'I'm glad that Jesus helped the blind man see. I want to say a thank you prayer. Thank you, Jesus, that you loved people. Thank you for helping the blind man to see'. You may then want to ask if any children would like to say a prayer, thanking God for our eyes. If several children want to pray, try to give them all a chance.

This may sound very guided to you. Children need to

learn to pray. They have heard many adults pray long, sometimes rambling prayers, and they may do the same without some clear guidance. In the context of a group of young children, short, directed prayers are probably best. It is not necessary to ask children to close their eyes, but you may want to suggest that sometimes. I tend to vary the way I pray. Sometimes I bow my head and close my eyes. Sometimes I look around at the children when I pray.

Children who are used to praying at home may tend to pray 'around the world'. Many have learned to do this at bedtime in order to stay up a bit later! If it appears that they are trying to pray for everything in one go, you may need to interrupt them gently, and ask them to finish their prayer so that someone else can have a turn. Again, it is a question of getting the right balance between encouraging children to pray, and at the same time, keeping other children's interest.

Now that we have considered what the elements of group time may be, let's look at how we might put them together. Firstly, we will consider some ideas for toddlers, then we will talk about three- and four-year-olds.

Group time for toddlers

The term 'toddler' may be loosely defined as a child who has started walking up to somewhere around the age of two. I have found that children who are between two and three can fit into a group time designed for toddlers, or into a group time for slightly older children. Where you put them depends on what the spread of ages is like, and how you divide your groups. In a setting of mixed ages, you may want to combine these ideas for younger children with ideas for three- and four-year-olds. Older children will accept some things that are aimed at toddlers, and younger children can at least observe some elements designed for older children. As you get to know the children you teach, you will discover what works best.

At the time of writing this, I am teaching a class of

toddlers in which the youngest child is 17 months and the oldest is 2½ years. I have found that a brief group time works well with them. If all the children were between one and two, that may not be the case. Sometimes you only discover what works by trial and error.

About ten to fifteen minutes before the end of the session, you can ask the children to help put things away. They require a large amount of help and supervision at this age, especially when bricks go in one bag, puzzles on a table and other toys in another bag! It is very tempting just to do it yourself, but helping to put things away is part of the teaching. It is the beginning of accepting responsibility. Once the toys are put away, you and the children can sit in a circle.

After a while, children learn the routine of things, so they know that after they put things away, they sit for group time. I use the same purple blanket every week. The children in my class know that we sit there together at the end. With children this age, you may find it helpful to give them a drink of juice. This helps them to sit down and remain relatively still. It is not a must, however. You could use a simple movement song or rhyme to get their attention and settle them down.

You may find it best to tell the story fairly soon after the children are seated. After only a few minutes, their attention wanders and they get restless. You can make the most of sixty seconds of quiet to tell them the Bible story. This is best done without any props or pictures. If you show a picture or use a doll or puppet, they will be so busy looking at your 'prop' that they will not hear the story. After you have told the story you may have a picture you can show.

The story will be short and simple for this age. Read it through several times before the session, and practise telling it without looking. The best way to hold the children's attention is by eye contact. Use variations in tone and volume of your voice to make the story live. It is not necessary to memorize what is written. Be able to tell it naturally, including all the important details.

At the end of the story you may want to pray or sing a song. Not many toddlers would be able to articulate a prayer, but it is good for them to hear the teacher pray.

You may want to use the rest of the time to look at the Bible, to sing songs or use movement rhymes. Always have some item planned for the last few minutes. In most churches, there is an approximate finishing time, but it varies by a few minutes each week. Use that time productively with dough, a ball or a game. Teaching does not stop until the last child has gone. If you have only one or two children left, you may want to ask them to help you finish tidying the room.

With toddlers, it is better to err on the side of a short group time, than to frustrate yourself and the children by trying to 'keep them entertained' for fifteen minutes at the end of the session. By the time the toys are put away and you sit down, you will only want to have about five minutes until the scheduled finishing time. In practice, this means you will actually have nearer ten minutes as you wait for parents and carers to collect children.

If you try group time with your toddlers and find that it is more of a trial than a benefit, do not worry. Leave it for a while, then try again in a few months. As long as you are teaching in the activities, they will not be 'cheated' by not having group time. We must remember that we want to build positive memories of times at church. We must be careful not to force children into group time before they are ready, simply because it fits within our adult definition of meaningful teaching.

Group time for three- and four-year-olds

The transition to group time with older under fives will be much the same as for toddlers. They, too, need to accept the responsibility of putting away the items they have been using during the session. You may want to give children who are in the middle of an activity a warning that it is nearly time to tidy up. 'Heather, it will be time to put things away in a minute. You will need to finish your painting'.

'Ryan, it will soon be time to put things away. When you have finished your puzzle, would you please put all the puzzles together in a pile?'

Giving children a warning about the time is a courtesy. It shows them that you know that what they are doing is important to them. Suddenly announcing that everyone must stop what they are doing and tidy up can be extremely frustrating to a child who is engrossed in an activity. They may then come to group time feeling cross rather than looking forward to it.

It is helpful to give children some direction about putting things away. You may want to give one child the bag for the bricks and then name two or three others to help him. In a room where there are several activity areas, a general admonition to 'tidy up' is too vague. Most children won't know where to start. They will be more co-operative if they are given a specific task to do. Sometimes singing about what a child is doing makes his job more tolerable (see 'Music' chapter, p. 172). (I think Mary Poppins knew something about that – a spoonful of sugar helps the medicine go down!)

Sometimes the children will come to group time and form themselves into a circle. If you always sit in the same part of the room, they become secure about where to go. From time to time you may want to make forming a circle into a game. You could suggest that the children stand together and as you sing their name they may come and sit down. It may help them if you move one place around the circle for each child, so they know to come and sit in front of your feet.

You may want to lead them around the room in a movement song on the way to the circle. You could sing, 'It's fun to walk around the room . . . around the room with our friends'. (To the tune of 'Here we go Round the Mulberry Bush') You could add march, skip or hop.

Once you are seated together for group time, you can use any combination of the elements suggested above. Every week you will want to have a Bible story, conversation and prayer. The other things you include will vary from week to week. Some weeks you may start with conversation, other weeks you may sing for a few minutes. When you are ready to tell the story, it is a good idea to let the children know that they need to be still and listen. I usually say something like, 'We have been doing lots of fun things, and we have been talking together. Now it is my turn to talk for a few minutes. I would like you to listen to what I have to tell you'. This will help to cut down on interruptions during the story.

Have the Bible open to the reference for the story. Although you will not be reading directly from the Bible, this is a visual aid to help children know that the story comes from the Bible, not some other book.

Tell the story naturally, without referring to notes, if possible. Maintain eye contact with the children. As with toddlers, props are not necessary. In fact, they can be a distraction. Because children find it hard to concentrate on more than one thing at a time, they will watch the prop rather than listen to the story. School-age children can listen and look at the same time, so they may be helped by the use of puppets or other aids. Under fives will take in the story and its significance more clearly if they hear it told simply and naturally, without any visual aids. You can hold their attention by varying the tone, volume and intensity of your voice. If you are interested in telling the story, they will be interested in listening.

When you have told the story, you may want to ask some questions to encourage conversation about the story as it relates to the theme. Using again the example of the story of Ruth and Naomi, you could say, 'Ruth helped Naomi find food to eat. Who cooks the food at your house, Anna?' This will prompt conversation about providing food. You could also say, 'Ruth wanted to stay with Naomi because she loved her and wanted to look after her. Robert, your mother and your grandmother love you and look after you. Who takes care of you, Michael?' (Remember that in conversations about home and family life it is helpful to know as much as you can about each child's situation. This enables you to include them without embarrassing them.)

Many times this kind of conversation leads quite naturally into prayer.

After the story you may want to use any number of Bible activities, games or music. You could provide some musical instruments for the children to play. These may be bought, or can be home-made, such as shakers and bells. It might be best to have only a few instruments and let the children take turns. If they are playing an instrument, they probably won't be able to sing as well. If only some of the children have an instrument, the others can sing. Probably it is better to wait until after the Bible story to use instruments, as they tend to increase the noise level, and it may be difficult to settle the children as quietly after that.

The key is a balance between security and variety. Children like to know that some things will be the same every week, hence the same location and always using the Bible with the story. But they also need some variety, so you would want to use different games, and sing a variety of songs, occasionally with instruments.

As with toddlers, it is good to keep the children involved in something even as they are being collected. If there are two teachers, one can stand at the door and quietly come and fetch a child from the circle as his parent arrives. This helps other children not to feel left behind, and also uses time productively. I have found that things soon dissolve into chaos at the end if you do not have something for the children to be interested in.

The length of group time will depend on the age mix and maturity level of the children. Having a shorter time in order to accommodate younger children is more effective than trying to prolong it for the older ones. If the toddlers are fidgeting, the three-year-olds won't be able to concentrate anyway. For a group of three- and four-year-olds you might think in terms of between ten and fifteen minutes. You will discover how long is best for the particular children you teach.

In a room where there is more than one teacher, it is probably better if the same teacher leads group time each week. No matter how closely two people are agreed on teaching style, they will still do group time quite differently. Having the same teacher lead group time each week gives a sense of routine. If the teacher uses variety, that strikes the balance mentioned earlier between security and change.

Before we conclude this section with some examples of songs, rhymes and Bible stories, a word about 'going home time' might be helpful. A good teaching session can end badly if the teacher never knows when to finish.

Some churches are very organized in their timetable, and finish within five minutes of the same time every week. This is very helpful for teachers of all ages, because they can plan accordingly. Other churches, however, have a more 'laid back' approach. I remember talking once to a lady who was working with under fives. She was very frustrated because the children went out during the sermon. Sometimes this was only about 15–20 minutes, other times it was 30 minutes. It was almost impossible for the teachers to plan. How can you start group time 15 minutes before the end if you have no idea when the end is? You might plan to have activities for 30 minutes and find the parents turning up after only twenty.

If this situation sounds familiar to you, it might be worth talking to your church leaders about it. It is likely that they don't realize how difficult variable timing makes things for those who teach the children. Think carefully about your present situation, then come up with a few suggestions for how you might solve the dilemma. If you can talk or write to a leader very positively with possible solutions, they will be much more willing to help you. Perhaps if they understand what you are trying to do, they will try to be more disciplined about time.

If there is not an immediate solution to the problem of timing, you may have to adapt. Perhaps you could have group time in the middle, then let children return to activities until the end. This means, of course, that they will not easily be able to help with the tidying up. It is better to do it yourself, though, and use your time most constructively.

Another problem that arises relates to who collects the children and how quickly. From time to time, parents need reminding to come and collect their children first, then return to the worship area to chat to people. Some parents send a brother or sister to collect an under five. Because we meet in a large school, which we must be very careful stewards of, I do not let children go with other children. I prefer to know that a child has gone with the appropriate adult. Very occasionally, I have had someone I do not know turn up at the door. They are family friends or relatives visiting for the day, and have come to collect a child while parents are talking. This has to be handled carefully. In all probability, they are who they say they are. But in these days, we have to be very careful of our children. I would rather embarrass myself, than let a child go with the wrong person.

These issues related to the end of the session will be handled differently in each church. There is not necessarily a right or wrong way to do things. So much depends on the size and location of the church, and the way the time is structured. They are issues that must be thought through carefully, so that teachers and leaders can work together to provide the best for everyone.

Sometimes the activity time goes brilliantly. The children respond eagerly to everything you do. Then group time is a disaster! Other times, the first part of the session is fraught with problems, but group time goes superbly. What a relief to know that the success of the morning does not depend on only one component.

Group time is an important part of the session, but it is not the most important part. Lack of teaching through activities is not made up for at the end by a ten minute group time. Nor does the occasional lacklustre group time negate what has gone on before. But good teaching through activities can be built upon and reinforced by a group time that is designed to meet the needs of the children.

Movement songs

Almost any combination of movements can be sung. The songs at the end of the chapter on music, on pp. 174–5, have simple tunes which may be adapted for other words. If you cannot read music, enlist the help of someone who can. Once you get the feel of the songs I have suggested, you will be able to make up a few of your own. When making up tunes for other words, remember to keep them simple and within the octave above middle C.

Don't worry about using these songs over and over again. Children seldom tire of a good movement song. In fact, they may ask to sing it every week, or more than once in any session!

Here are some other words that children enjoy:

> Snap, snap, snap your fingers,
> Tap, tap, tap your toes.
> Clap, clap, clap your hands
> Then turn around while the music goes.

> Hopping is fun, O hopping is fun,
> Hopping is fun for everyone.
> The more you hop, the better you hop,
> So keep on hopping up and down.

(You can add marching . . . all around, skipping . . . round and round, jumping . . . up and down)

Movement rhymes

> I touch my hair, my lips, my eyes.
> I sit up straight, and then I rise.
> I touch my toes, my knees, my chin,
> Then quietly sit down again.

This rhyme involves opening and closing your fingers into a fist:

Open, shut them, open, shut them,
Hold them very tight. (Squeeze both
    hands together.)
Open, shut them, open, shut them,
Shake them out so light. (Shake both
    hands gently.)

Or you can vary the one above:

Open, shut them, open, shut them,
Give a little clap.
Open, shut them, open, shut them,
Put them in your lap.

Sometimes I'm tall, (Stand and stretch
    arms above head.)
Sometimes I'm small. (Stoop down low.)
Sometimes tall, sometimes small,
And sometimes, I'm just myself again.
    (Stand normally.)

These are a few possibilities – there are many others.
When you are comfortable with these, try making up some
of your own.

Bible stories

The following examples show possible ways of
paraphrasing Bible stories to suit different age groups.

Since we have used the story of Ruth and Naomi as an
illustration, perhaps we should start with that one. This
would be appropriate for three- and four-year-olds.

Ruth and Naomi

A woman named Naomi lived with her husband and two
sons in a country called Judah. One year there was not
enough food to eat in that country. Naomi and her family
were hungry. Her husband said, 'We will move to Moab.
There is enough food there'. So they went to live in a
place called Moab. While they were there, Naomi's

husband died. Her two sons got married – one married Ruth, and the other married Orpah. After many years, Naomi's sons died. Naomi wanted to go back and live in her own country. There was plenty of food there now. She set off with Ruth and Orpah, but then she said to them, 'You do not need to come with me. Moab is your country. You can stay here – maybe you will be more happy'. After they talked about it, Orpah decided to stay in Moab. But Ruth said, 'I do not want to leave you, Naomi. I want to live in your country. I want to love God like you do. I will look after you. I am part of your family'. So Naomi and Ruth went back to Judah together. Ruth found grain for Naomi to make bread. Ruth took care of Naomi.

If you want to use the story with older toddlers and two-year-olds, you can leave out some of the detail:

Naomi's family were hungry. There was not enough food in their country. Naomi's husband said, 'We will move to Moab. There is enough food there'. So they went to live in Moab. While they were there, Naomi's husband died. Her two sons got married – one married Ruth, and the other married Orpah. After many years, Naomi's sons died. Naomi heard that there was food in her own country now. She wanted to go back there and live. Orpah decided to stay in Moab. But Ruth said, 'I do not want to leave you, Naomi. I want to live in your country. I want to love God like you do. I will look after you. I am part of your family'. So Naomi and Ruth went back to Naomi's country together. Ruth found grain for Naomi to make bread. Ruth took care of Naomi.

You may want to follow on with the theme of families caring for each other by continuing the story the next week:

Ruth and Boaz
Ruth went to the fields of grain to pick up the pieces that the workers left behind. She and Naomi would use the

grain to make flour, so they could bake bread to eat. The field belonged to a kind man named Boaz. He saw Ruth gathering grain. 'You may come to my fields every day. I will tell my workers to let you gather grain. You will be safe in my fields'. After a while, Boaz married Ruth. They had a baby boy. Grandmother Naomi was very happy. The women came to visit her and said, 'You must be very glad to have a grandson. God has taken care of you and Ruth. Ruth loves you and has looked after you well'. The baby's name was Obed. Perhaps Grandmother Naomi helped Ruth and Boaz look after baby Obed. Perhaps she said, 'Thank you, God, for my grandson'. Naomi was glad that she had a family to be with.

For toddlers and two-year-olds:

Ruth picked up grain from a field. She and Naomi would use it to bake bread that they could eat. The field belonged to a kind man named Boaz. After a while, Boaz married Ruth. They had a baby boy. Grandmother Naomi was very happy. The women came to visit her and said, 'You must be very glad to have a grandson. God has taken care of you and Ruth. Ruth loves you and has looked after you well'. The baby's name was Obed. Perhaps Grandmother Naomi helped Ruth and Boaz look after baby Obed. Perhaps she said, 'Thank you, God, for my grandson'. Naomi was glad that she had a family to be with.

Jesus teaches about God's care (Matthew 6:25–33)

Wherever Jesus went, people followed him. Many of them liked to listen to the things he said. One day, Jesus was sitting outside, teaching the people. He said to them, 'Look up at the birds in the sky. They do not have to work hard to make food. But God provides food for them to eat. He loves the birds, but he loves you even more'. Then he looked at all the flowers growing in the field. He said, 'Look at all these flowers. They do not have to sew to make clothes for themselves. But even kings dressed up in all their best clothes are not as beautiful as the flowers. God loves the flowers, but he loves you even more. God takes care of the flowers, and he will take care of you, too. The most important thing is for you to love God, and do the things that please him. He will take care of you'.

For toddlers and two-year-olds:

One day, Jesus was sitting outside teaching the people. He said, 'Look at the birds in the sky. God loves the birds, but he loves you even more. God takes care of the birds and he will take care of you'. Then Jesus looked at the fields, and said, 'Look at all the beautiful flowers. God loves the flowers, but he loves you even more. God takes care of the flowers, and he will take care of you. The most important thing is to love God and do the things that make him happy. God will take care of you'.

Jesus and Bartimaeus

Bartimaeus sat by the side of the road. He could hear the footsteps on the dusty road as many people walked by. He could hear the sound of their voices, talking and laughing. But he could not see them. Bartimaeus was blind. He called out to the people walking past him, 'What is happening?' Someone told him that Jesus was walking past. Bartimaeus had heard about Jesus. He knew that Jesus could make people well. 'Jesus', he called out, 'Jesus, please help me'. Some of the people told him to be quiet, but he shouted even louder, 'Jesus, please help me!' Jesus heard Bartimaeus, and said, 'Tell the man who is calling to come to me'. The people said, 'Quick, Bartimaeus. Jesus is asking for you'. They led him to Jesus. 'What would you like me to do to help you?' asked Jesus. 'I want to be able to see,' said Bartimaeus. 'It is good that you believe I can make you well', said Jesus, 'You can go now'. As soon as Jesus said that, Bartimaeus could see again. Bartimaeus had been blind. Jesus helped him to see again.

(This story lends itself to good conversation with three-

and four-year-olds. What would it be like to be blind? Close your eyes and cover them with your hand. How do you think Bartimaeus would have felt after Jesus made him see? Do you think he would have been glad? These kinds of statements and questions help the children to understand the significance of what Jesus did.)

For toddlers and two-year-olds:

Bartimaeus sat by the side of the road. He could hear, but he could not see. He was blind. He heard the sounds of many people walking past him. He called out, 'What is happening?' Someone told him, 'It is Jesus. Jesus is coming this way!' Bartimaeus had heard about Jesus. He knew that Jesus could make him see again. He shouted, 'Jesus, please help me!' Jesus heard him, and asked the people to bring Bartimaeus to him. 'What would you like me to do for you?' Jesus asked. 'Please, Jesus, I want to be able to see', said Bartimaeus. 'You knew that I could make you well', said Jesus. 'Now you can see'. As soon as Jesus said that, Bartimaeus was able to see again. Jesus had made him well.

These examples will help you to see how you can tell Bible stories accurately, but in language that young children can understand. Try rephrasing some yourself. Here are some suggested stories:
● God made the world   Genesis 1
● God made people   Genesis 1 and 2
● Miriam helps care for baby Moses   Exodus 2:1–10
● King Josiah repairs the church and reads the Bible to the people   2 Kings 22:1–20, 23:1–3
● Jesus is born   Luke 2:1–7
● Shepherds visit baby Jesus   Luke 2:8–20
● Simeon and Anna see Jesus   Luke 2:22–40
● Jesus goes to church   Luke 2:40–51
● Four men take their friend to see Jesus   Mark 2:1–12
● The man who said thank you   Luke 17:11–19
● Jesus and the children   Matthew 19:13–15, Mark 10:13–16, Luke 18:15–17

- A boy shares his lunch (or, Jesus feeds the people) John 6:1–13
- Jesus visits friends Luke 10:38–42
- Paul works with Aquila and Priscilla Acts 18:1–4
- Philip tells a man about Jesus Acts 8:26–35

A last word

Teaching the under fives at church (and at home) is only a part of building for God's future. I believe it is a very important part. We may never be able to measure the results of all our work in this area. Teenagers or adults who are committed to serving the Lord may not even remember the adults who taught and influenced them before they were five. But my experience shows me that among Christian teenagers and adults, the most mature spiritually are often the ones who have known the things of God from a very early age.

The children that you and I have in our charge, as parents, teachers or care-givers, are growing up in a rapidly changing world. God has given us the privilege and the responsibility to prepare them not only for the next century, but for a new millenium.

What do we need to teach them to equip them for the future? What do they need to know in order to fulfil God's purposes in their lives? How can we help them to grow up into men and women of God?

In our changing world there are very few certainties. As Christians we have an unchanging, faithful God, who has given us his Word for our lives. What better foundation can we build into the lives of our children than to help them know, obey and love this Word?

Remember the vision we spoke of in the early pages of this book? That you and I might see a generation of children who have never known anything but to love the Lord? It will take a long time to see the fulfilment of this vision. We may never know how many lives have been touched by our loving consistent teaching. The measure of our service for God lies not in visible results, but in our faithfulness to what he has called us to do.

My mother teaches conferences in the United States for

teachers of under fives in the church. She often uses this little poem:

> I saw tomorrow look at me
>   through little childrens' eyes,
> And thought how carefully we'd teach
>   if we were really wise.

Through the under fives you and I have an opportunity to touch and change tomorrow. May God help us to be faithful, and give us a passion for passing on a living, active faith to our children.

Further reading

In preparing this manuscript I have read many books about children in general, and under fives specifically. Most of them are published abroad and are not available in Britain. Many of them are so specific to the culture in which they were written that they would not easily 'translate'.

In Britain you will be able to read a number of books about children in the church, and children learning about God. Many of these are very good and helpful, but they deal mainly with children aged six to eleven. Hence this very short list of books I can recommend that are written about under fives!

Under Fives and Their Families, Judith Wigley. A CPAS Handbook (Marshall Pickering, 1990).
Teaching Young Children (Everything you Want to Know About . . .), Wesley Haystead (Gospel Light Publications, 1989).
Under Fives Welcome!, Kathleen Crawford (Scripture Union, 1990).

UNDERSTANDING TEENAGERS

Pete Gilbert

Teenagers!
Sometimes they are lovable . . .
Sometimes they drive us crazy . . .

Often we simply do not know how to relate to our teenagers. This guide by Pete Gilbert shows us how. He teaches us to understand teenagers, how they think, react, feel. Young people face pressures that we never knew and this book deftly guides us through the jungle.

Understanding Teenagers is essential reading for today's parents, and will also be invaluable for youth-group leaders and pastors.

Pete Gilbert is one of Britain's leading experts on teenagers, with many years of experience with British Youth for Christ and now with TIE teams. A regular speaker at events such as Spring Harvest, he has also written several books, including the bestselling *Teenage Survival Kit*. Pete and his family work with the Revelation Fellowship.

THE ENGAGED COUPLES HANDBOOK

Mike and Katey Morris

Getting married? This helpful handbook has all you need to know.

The **A–Z** format is especially designed to help find the answers to all those tricky questions! It tells you all you need to know about the wedding, sex, and how to get on with the in-laws, along with a whole host of other practical details.

There are useful charts to help you run your home more effectively, and keep out of debt; questionnaires for both partners to fill in will help with getting to know about one another before the wedding.

Mike and Katey Morris are regular speakers at marriage seminars and prepare numerous couples for marriage. They are the authors of the bestseller *Praying Together*. Mike is the International Secretary of the EA and a leader with Revelation Church in Chichester; and Katey is a primary schoolteacher.

PROPHET
A NOVEL
Frank E. Peretti

' You will know the truth, and the truth will set you free' (John 8: 32)

John Barrett, anchorman for 'NewsSix at Five', the city's most watched newscast, has a problem. His comfortable, successful world is being jarred to breaking point. He's caught his producer skewing a story to fit her own prejudices, then lying to cover her tracks – and she appears to be hiding something much bigger. His father's 'accidental' death suddenly isn't looking so accidental. Carl, his estranged son, has returned to challenge his integrity and probe to find the man behind the TV image. The supposedly professional and objective newsroom is now divided and fighting over Truth. And what are these mysterious 'voices' Barrett is hearing ...?

Once again, master storyteller **Frank Peretti** has woven a prophetic tale for our times. *Prophet* carries all the hallmarks of Frank's blockbusting fiction – plenty of edge-of-the-seat action, nail-biting suspense, breakneck pacing, and blow-you-out-of-the-water spiritual impact. But more than this, it penetrates to the very heart of a vast struggle that threatens to tear our society to pieces, the struggle over which vision of moral authority will define our nation.

David Watson, J I Packer, Derick Bingham, Michael Baughen, Edward England, Jean Darnall, J. Oswald Sanders, Selwyn Hughes, Phyllis Thompson, Jean Wilson, Richard Wurmbrand.

A PASSION FOR HOLINESS
J. I. Packer

Changing our lives for the better

The sequel to *Keep in Step with the Spirit.*

'This will take our best thinking and our most faithful living.'

Richard Foster

'No one is better qualified to address this call.'

Chuck Colson

As Christians succumb more and more to materialism, holiness is becoming the forgotten virtue of the Church. Yet, as the Bible makes clear, holiness is high on God's priorities for his people.

J. I. Packer brings us back to where God wants us to be. He shows us that holiness is nothing less than a lifelong passion for loving God and following his ways.

J. I. Packer is Professor of Systematic and Historical Theology at Regent College, Vancouver, Canada, and has also held posts in his native Britain. Dr. Packer is the author of numerous best-sellers including *Knowing God, Keep in Step with the Spirit* and most recently *Among God's Giants.*

ACTS

Stephen Gaukroger

Free to live

Crossway Bible Guides

Series Editor for the New Testament: Ian Coffey

Acts is one of the most exciting and relevant Bible books for Christians today. It shows us God powerfully at work in the early church.

This invaluable study guide enables us to find out how Acts speaks to us now. There is plenty of application, so that we can put into practice the lessons we learn in each study.

The Crossway Bible Guides are specially designed for home-group study and for readers at all levels of ability.
Each section has:
   A detailed explanation of the passage
   Questions for group and personal study.

Some sections also have special features that explain complex passages in greater depth.

Stephen Gaukroger is one of Britain's best-known speakers, and the author of bestsellers such as *It Makes Sense*. The Senior Minister of a church in Bedfordshire, he was the youngest ever elected President of the Baptist Union. He and his wife Janet have three children.